Praise for *Invincible*

"Are you having difficulty believing you are a conqueror in Jesus Christ? In *Invincible* you will be encouraged to face the big mountains in your life and learn to live a life of boldness for God. You will benefit significantly from Dr. Jeffress's biblical insights on how to overcome doubt, guilt, anxiety, discouragement, fear, bitterness, materialism, loneliness, lust, and grief that are ravishing your life."

Jason Jimenez, founder of Stand Strong Ministries
and bestselling author of *Challenging Conversations*

"There is often pressure in church to act as if you have it all together. 'Don't bring your doubt, anxiety, fear, or guilt in this place!' *Invincible* pushes back against this kind of phony faith and gives us the freedom to acknowledge our struggles. With humor, compassion, and practical advice, Dr. Jeffress provides a way to overcome the mountains we all face and encourage one another on our faith journey. This book is for real people who want real change."

Michael C. Sherrard, pastor and author of *Why You Matter*

Praise for *Courageous*

"With all the uncertainty in our world right now, this new book by my friend Robert Jeffress is a welcome encouragement for believers. His Bible-based tips on thriving during challenging times are not only practical and easy to understand but will help you to stand strong in your faith and live victoriously."

Robert Morris, founding and lead senior pastor of Gateway Church and
bestselling author of *The Blessed Life*, *Frequency*, and *Beyond Blessed*

"When it comes to living out biblical principles, we quickly discover we're in an unfriendly culture. Ephesians 5:11 tells us to 'Have nothing to do with the fruitless deeds of darkness,' so how then do we build bridges to skeptics and cynics? How do we win wicked people with antagonistic agendas to the side of our Savior? In his remarkable new book, *Courageous: 10 Strategies for Thriving in a Hostile World*, Dr. Jeffress shows us page-by-page how to live as winsome and effective ambassadors for Jesus Christ, all so that the perishing will come to salvation and God will receive the glory! I give this book a double thumbs-up!"

Joni Eareckson Tada, Joni and Friends International Disability Center

"No book title ever fit its author's personality better than this one. One of the words I often use to describe Robert Jeffress is *courageous*. As a former pastor of First Baptist in Dallas, I have been privileged to watch time and again his courageous yet loving leadership in daily action. This book is not some self-help treatise. These principles have been beaten out on the anvil of the author's own personal and practical experience. Read it . . . and reap!

O. S. Hawkins, former pastor of First Baptist Church in Dallas and author of the bestselling Code series of Christian devotionals

"My friend Robert Jeffress has demonstrated courage time and again by boldly preaching God's Word in the pulpit and answering tough critics in the media. In these pages, he outlines practical survival strategies that will help us courageously navigate the storms of life. Through powerful biblical examples and present-day testimonies, Robert reminds us that the wisdom and supernatural ability God has provided us as believers are more than enough to defeat the enemy's strategy."

James Robison, founder and president of LIFE Outreach International, Fort Worth, Texas

Praise for *Choosing the Extraordinary Life*

"Biblical, relevant, and very straightforward. Dr. Jeffress has written a remarkable and on-time book about the seven secrets to 'finding, keeping, and living' an extraordinary life. His unique approach and practical insights will guide you on a new and fresh journey, leading you away from any distractions that would keep you from intimacy and favor with your loving heavenly Father."

Marcus D. Lamb, founder and president of Daystar Television Network

"Dr. Jeffress brings Scripture alive with the truth God's Spirit put into it. If you like rich, useful Bible teaching, you'll appreciate this book. Jeffress wisely unpacks seven secrets from Elijah's life and ministry for leading the life we were meant to live. No formulas or pat answers here. Depend on this book to guide you on the narrow road that leads to life."

Dr. Larry Crabb, psychologist, Bible teacher, and author of *When God's Ways Make No Sense*

"We love this book! It's a must-read for every Christian. Thank you, Dr. Jeffress, for inspiring and challenging us to rise above the status quo of this world. *Choosing the Extraordinary Life* is one of those books that's honest, motivating, and life-changing. If you want to live a life that's truly worth living, the seven secrets inside this book will show you how. Your life will never be the same again."

Kristen Clark and Bethany Baird, cofounders of GirlDefined Ministries and authors of *Girl Defined* and *Love Defined*

INVINCIBLE

CONQUERING THE MOUNTAINS
THAT SEPARATE YOU
FROM THE BLESSED LIFE

DR. ROBERT JEFFRESS

BakerBooks
a division of Baker Publishing Group
Grand Rapids, Michigan

Published by Baker Books
a division of Baker Publishing Group
PO Box 6287, Grand Rapids, MI 49516-6287
www.bakerbooks.com

Printed in the United States of America

Library of Congress Cataloging-in-Publication Data
Names: Jeffress, Robert, 1955– author.
Title: Invincible : conquering the mountains that separate you from the blessed life / Robert Jeffress.
Description: Grand Rapids, Michigan : Baker Books, a division of Baker Publishing Group, [2021] | Includes bibliographical references.
Identifiers: LCCN 2021003779 | ISBN 9780801075407 (cloth) | ISBN 9781493432875 (ebook)
Subjects: LCSH: Christian life. | Self-actualization (Psychology)—Religious aspects—Christianity.
Classification: LCC BV4501.3 .J444 2021 | DDC 248.4—dc23
LC record available at https://lccn.loc.gov/2021003779

Published in association with Yates & Yates, www.yates2.com.

21 22 23 24 25 26 27   7 6 5 4 3 2 1

To Carrilyn Baker

Amy and I are eternally grateful
to you for all you have done to help me,
our church, and Pathway to Victory as my executive
assistant for more than twenty years.
Thank you for continuing to serve God tirelessly
and cheerfully through your ministry.

CONTENTS

ACKNOWLEDGMENTS

MOUNTAIN CLIMBING requires teamwork. Mountaineers generally link together with a safety rope and help one another across challenging terrain. To summit a mountain, a team of climbers, logistics managers, and porters must all work together to achieve their goal. The success of any mountain climbing expedition depends entirely on the team.

The same is true when it comes to conquering the mountain of writing a book. Any book that completes the journey from an idea to the printed page is a result of the cooperation, support, and expertise of a successful team. That's why I'm eternally grateful for the exceptionally talented team God has given me:

Brian Vos, Mark Rice, Brianna DeWitt, Lindsey Spoolstra, and the rest of the team at Baker Books, the best publishing partner I've ever worked with.

Derrick G. Jeter, creative director of Pathway to Victory, and Jennifer Stair, who diligently assisted in crafting and polishing the message of this book.

Sealy Yates, my literary agent and friend, whose wise counsel and consistent encouragement have helped me for more than two decades.

Carrilyn Baker, my extraordinary executive associate, who expertly coordinates the complicated work of our office with a joyful spirit. And thank you, Mary Shafer, for tirelessly assisting Carrilyn and me in so many ways!

Ben Lovvorn, executive pastor of First Baptist Church, Dallas, and Nate Curtis, Patrick Heatherington, Ben Bugg, and the entire Pathway to Victory team, who extend the message of this book to millions of people around the world.

I'm deeply grateful for the support I receive every day from my greatest team—my family. God has blessed me with two wonderful daughters, Julia and Dorothy, a great son-in-law, Ryan Sadler, and my beloved triplet grandchildren, Barrett, Blake, and Blair.

And at the very top of the list of people who have helped me conquer mountains and provided consistent support and encouragement is my wife of forty-five years, Amy. Thank you for your unconditional love. You are God's greatest blessing of goodness and grace.

PREPARING TO CONQUER
YOUR MOUNTAINS

RISING TO 29,029 FEET, Mount Everest is the tallest mountain on earth. Located along a plateau popularly known as "the roof of the world," this imposing peak has captivated mountain climbers for decades, beckoning them to stand on its summit.

On May 29, 1953, mountaineers Edmund Hillary and Tenzing Norgay became the first explorers to scale Mount Everest. But it wasn't Hillary's first attempt. After failing to reach the summit two years earlier, Hillary reportedly shook his fist at the mountain and said, "I will come again and conquer you because as a mountain you can't grow, but as a human, I can."[1]

Hillary had learned a valuable lesson. A mountain that seems insurmountable isn't—as long as we're willing to grow. And with growth comes a change in perspective and a renewed hope that, in the days to come, even Everest-like mountains can and will be conquered.

Chances are you and I will never climb a literal mountain like Everest, but we will come face-to-face with other tall mountains in our lives. The mountain looming over us may be called doubt or discouragement. Perhaps we are blocked by a daunting mountain of bitterness or guilt. Or we may find ourselves in the shadow of a seemingly insurmountable mountain of loneliness or grief.

Like Everest, the mountains you and I face in life can seem overwhelming. But we're not meant to cower in fear and defeat. With God on our side, we're meant to be invincible! That's why Jesus said, "Have faith in God. Truly I say to you, whoever says to this mountain, 'Be taken up and cast into the sea,' and does not doubt in his heart, but believes that what he says is going to happen, it will be granted him" (Mark 11:22–23).

Move That Mountain

The biblical writers often used the imagery of a mountain to refer to something that seemed impossible. In the Old Testament book of Zechariah, for example, an angel said to the prophet, "What are you, O great mountain? Before Zerubbabel you will become a plain" (4:7).

Seventy years earlier, Nebuchadnezzar's army had marched into Jerusalem and destroyed Solomon's magnificent temple. When the Jews finally returned to their homeland, rebuilding the temple to its former glory seemed impossible. But the angel promised Zechariah that God would level that "great mountain" like "a plain." How? "'Not by might nor by power, but by My Spirit,' says the LORD of hosts" (v. 6).

Just as the Israelites faced what seemed like a mountain in rebuilding God's temple, you and I also face mountains in life that threaten to defeat us. Not long ago, my family faced our own mountain. My older daughter, Julia, and her husband, Ryan, suffered three devastating miscarriages in less than a year. My wife, Amy, and I joined them in continually asking the Lord for a viable pregnancy and a healthy baby. But God chose not to answer those prayers . . . until Julia got pregnant with our triplet grandchildren, who have brought us immeasurable joy. Why didn't God answer our earlier prayers? Was it because we didn't have enough faith? No! Though we sometimes doubted God's timing and His methods, we knew that God loved Julia and Ryan, and if it was His will for them to have natural-born children, then He would make a way through the mountain of infertility and keeping a pregnancy. When the triplets were born, we knew that, with God, we had been invincible over that mountain. This experience strengthened our faith and reminded us that from God's perspective, even the tallest mountain is but a speck in His hand.

In Matthew 17, Jesus said, "Truly I say to you, if you have faith the size of a mustard seed, you will say to this mountain, 'Move from here to there,' and it will move; and nothing will be impossible to you" (v. 20). Jesus wasn't referring to physical mountains. He was using imagery to communicate a spiritual truth: all of us will encounter mountain-like difficulties in life that seem overwhelming. Bible scholar William Barclay explained this well: "What Jesus meant was: 'If you have faith enough, all difficulties can be solved, and even the hardest task can be accomplished.' Faith in God is the instrument which enables men and women to remove hills of difficulty which block their path."[2]

Notice Jesus didn't say it takes mountain-sized faith to move mountains; it takes only mustard seed–sized faith.

Mustard seeds are tiny. Jesus wanted His disciples (and us) to understand that God will honor even the smallest amount of faith. When we put our faith in God and rely on His power, praying according to His will, He will enable us to shake our fists at the mountains in our lives and say, "I will conquer you because I am growing in my faith—and by faith, God will help me be invincible!"

The Mountain Mover

At first glance, mustard seed faith hardly seems enough to conquer the mountains that loom large in our lives. But to look at the mountains from merely a human viewpoint is to take our eyes off the Mountain Mover. The ancient Israelites did that when they looked across the river into the promised land.

In Numbers 13, God's people were on the verge of receiving the blessing promised long ago. All they had to do was cross the river and conquer the people who lived there. But when the spies Moses sent in to survey the land returned, ten of the twelve were frightened by the mountain-sized people who occupied the land. They were so large, these spies said, "We became like grasshoppers in our own sight" (v. 33).

Can't you picture the image? People as big as mountains compared to people as small as grasshoppers. From the spies' perspective, the mountain-sized giants could (and would) squash them like bugs. What the spies failed to consider was that the God who made the mountains had already promised to move the mountains, if they would just have faith and trust His promise.

Moving the Mountains in Your Life

Standing at the base of a mountain that blocks your path feels daunting. But instead of looking at the crevasses and rocks, you can choose to focus on what awaits you on the other side. When you learn to do that, your mountains won't seem intimidating anymore.

Invincible was written to help you do just that. This book describes ten of the most difficult mountains that can separate you from the blessed life God has for you. Each chapter will equip you with biblical insights and practical tools so that, when the mountain you face threatens to defeat you, you can conquer it and come out stronger on the other side.

Moving from Doubt to Faith

When we encounter the mountain of doubt, it blocks our view of God's grace, mercy, and love. Doubt can lead to uncertainty about the truth of Scripture and even our salvation. Conquering this mountain requires an act of faith. When we confront our doubts with the truth of God's Word, we can confidently climb the rocky and steep places in life with a renewed faith.

Moving from Guilt to Repentance

Past sins, unrepented sins, and secret sins lead us to the vast mountain of guilt. As a result, we avoid God, His Word, and His people. Overwhelmed by guilt and shame, we believe we are unworthy of God's love and think He can never use us again. But this isn't true. Carrying guilt is like carrying a heavy load of useless equipment on a mountain climb. The minute we drop that weight by repenting of our sin, we feel lighter spiritually and mentally. We can then proceed to do all God has for us to do with a clear conscience.

Moving from Anxiety to Peace

When we come to the mountain of anxiety, we wonder why God isn't doing something about the wrongs in the world or the difficulties in our lives. We ask, "Why hasn't God made things right? Why hasn't He answered my prayers?" Like getting lost in the mountains, anxiety causes confusion and prevents us from moving forward with purpose. At times like these, we need to take a deep breath and reorient ourselves to focus on God. When we do, we will discover His lasting, supernatural peace.

Moving from Discouragement to Hope

With anxiety come discouragement, disappointment, and depression. The mountain of discouragement can drop us into a deep, dark crevasse that seems impossible to climb out of. But God's Word provides a lifeline for those caught in depression, lifting us out of the black hole we find ourselves in and placing us on the sunlit path of hope.

Moving from Fear to Courage

The fear of insignificance, rejection, failure, poverty, illness, and death can stop us in our tracks. But if we are to experience the blessed life Jesus promised (John 10:10), then, with His help, we must conquer the mountain of fear. When we're standing at its base the mountain may seem unnerving, but after we take the first step, we'll find renewed courage.

Moving from Bitterness to Forgiveness

Not all anger is sinful (Eph. 4:26). But bitterness, resentment, unforgiveness, and revenge are. These attitudes are like avalanches or rockslides; they will batter us heart and soul. The mountain of bitterness can make us as hard as granite, affecting those around us as well. This isn't the life God intends for us, so we must learn to surmount this mountain with forgiveness.

Moving from Materialism to Contentment

Somehow we've Christianized the mountain of materialism, which often starts with the subtle sin of greed and leads to the not-so-subtle problems of debt and financial instability. We can become consumed with the pursuit of *more*, which grinds and crushes our souls. It is then that we must learn one of the hardest lessons the Bible has to teach—contentment.

Moving from Loneliness to Companionship

Intimate, enduring relationships have always been complicated, but today they are even more challenging to maintain. In an age of social media, virtual friends are made and lost at the click of a button. And as we get older, we can become increasingly disconnected from friends, family members, and church, causing us to face the mountain of loneliness. In times like these, we must shore up our hearts by pursuing companionship.

Moving from Lust to Purity

The mountain of lust isn't only about sex. Lust is burning after anything apart from God's will. It's a self-absorbed desire to fulfill the appetites that tempt us, whether sexual or otherwise. The only sure way to move this mountain is through a recommitment to purity—doing God's will in every aspect of our lives.

Moving from Grief to Acceptance

The mountain of grief can come with the passing of a loved one, the end of a marriage, infertility or miscarriage, a broken friendship, the death of a dream, or the termination of a career. Though grief is a natural process we go through after a loss, if we allow ourselves to set up camp instead of confronting this mountain, we can become paralyzed by depression and despair. We may not be able to eliminate grief, but we can keep it from controlling our lives as we come to the point of accepting what is lost and starting to move forward.

The Grandeur of Your Life

My father was an amateur mountain climber. Though I didn't inherit his interest in mountaineering, I can appreciate the majesty of mountains. Their snow-capped peaks loom large on the landscape, causing us to wonder at our all-powerful God.

Mountains humble us. But even the tallest mountain stands in humility before God, who helps us overcome the mountain-like difficulties in our lives. In the little book of Nahum, the prophet wrote, "Mountains quake because of Him and the hills dissolve; indeed the earth is upheaved by His presence" (1:5).

Every one of us has faced at least one of the ten mountains we'll explore in this book, and if you haven't, chances are you know someone who has. If you and I ever hope to conquer these mountains and experience the blessed life God wants us to live, then we must step out in faith with our eyes fully fixed on the One whose presence causes mountains to melt like wax (Ps. 97:5). Mark Batterson has written beautifully about this: "It's the mountains we overcome that make us who we are! The inclination is to curse the mountains in our path or try to avoid them altogether. . . . Don't be too quick to curse the challenges you face, because God may be preparing you for something bigger, something better!"[3]

Your mountain looms before you. But fear not—though you will encounter many challenges in life that threaten to defeat you, God meant for you to be invincible! Every mountain you face is merely a molehill to the Mountain Mover, who has the blessed life waiting for you on the other side.

ONE

MOVING FROM
DOUBT TO FAITH

———

WHEN I WAS NINETEEN YEARS OLD, I was in college studying to be a pastor. But after listening to some of the professors in the classes I was taking, I began having doubts about the trustworthiness of the Bible. I remember thinking, *Is the Bible really the Word of God? How can I commit my life to preaching the Word if I'm not even sure the Bible is true? Should I even go into ministry?*

Then the respected evangelist Billy Graham came to preach at our church. I was excited about the opportunity to listen to his message. That evening, Dr. Graham spoke about his early years in the ministry and admitted to having similar doubts about the Bible when he was around my age. He described one night on a mountain trail when he set his Bible on a tree stump and cried out, "Father, I am going to accept this as Thy Word—by faith! I'm going to allow faith to go beyond my intellectual questions and doubts, and I will believe this to be Your inspired Word!"[1] He said that decision transformed his life and his ministry.

When I heard Billy Graham talk about his struggle with doubt, I made that same commitment in my heart, and I could feel my faith growing stronger. I recommitted my life to believing and preaching the truth of God's Word.

Later that evening, I ran into Dr. Graham and told him about my commitment. He congratulated me and wrote a note in my Bible that I'll treasure forever. His genuine care for me at a time when I was wrestling with doubt impacted my life in a very meaningful way and affirmed to me that God's Word is true. God is who He says He is.

We All Doubt

Faith is like a day in the sunshine. But doubt is like a shadow that blocks the sun and sends a shiver through our souls. Unfortunately, on this side of heaven, doubts are inevitable. None of us is exempt. In fact, some of God's choicest servants went through periods of deep doubt. Moses doubted his ability as a deliverer, David doubted God would rescue him from King Saul, Elijah doubted he would survive Queen Jezebel's hit squad, and Jeremiah doubted his call as a prophet. And it would take many pages to detail the doubts of Solomon, John the Baptist, and the apostle Paul—to say nothing of Martin Luther, John Calvin, D. L. Moody, Amy Carmichael, Joni Eareckson Tada, and many other respected Christian men and women through the centuries.

Many believers today find themselves face-to-face with the imposing mountain of doubt, which can block their view of

God. Countless Christian students go to college and return home, as I did, with doubts about what they were taught concerning the Bible, creation, God, and the resurrection. Many Christian parents pray fervently for their prodigal children to return to the Lord but instead encounter additional rebellion, leading these parents to wonder whether God really exists or if He's really good and loving. And believers face illnesses that take the lives of loved ones and think, *Is this how God deals with those who love and follow Him?* Sometimes, yes.

I'm convinced that those who don't doubt much are those who don't think much or experience much. Airtight conclusions usually come from people who haven't known the sting of disappointment or the confusion of unanswered prayers. The truth is, life is too big for us to have it all worked out. There are many things we simply don't understand.

Nevertheless, some Christians think we should have the mysteries of life and faith neatly wrapped up in a box with a tag that reads "Off-limits for doubts and questions." Those who think this way are either cutting themselves off from the real world or setting themselves up for a serious dose of reality. At the heart of such thinking is fear; they are afraid to be vulnerable and honest, even with themselves. No one has life all figured out. All of us have questions, and when our questions go unanswered or the answers elude our grasp, we face the mountain of doubt.

Doubt versus Unbelief

Most of us have gone through times when what God is doing in our lives confounds us. The plans we have for our lives don't square with what's actually happening in our lives, and our faith flounders. It seems like God is ignoring our prayers or telling us just to deal with it. Either way, God is taking us places we'd just as soon not go. At times like these, we think, *Why doesn't God consult me? Why doesn't He show me the big picture?*

In Isaiah 55:8, the Lord said, "My thoughts are not your thoughts, nor are your ways My ways." In fact, the distance between His thoughts and ways and our thoughts and ways is so great that the Lord declared, "For as the heavens are higher than the earth, so are My ways higher than your ways and My thoughts than your thoughts" (v. 9). God doesn't surrender His sovereignty to what we think He should do. He's the potter and we are the clay; He can mold us into anything He desires (64:8). And because He is God (and we're not), He exercises His will to accomplish whatever He chooses in our lives. It may not be what we wanted or hoped for, but it will be exactly what we need.

"That sounds very spiritual, Pastor," you may be saying, "but telling me that God's ways are greater than my ways doesn't get rid of my doubts. In fact, that's the whole reason for my doubts. God's ways are sometimes so doggone confusing."

I agree—they are. If your doubts cause you to run to God with sincere questions about what He is doing (or not doing), then asking is an act of faith. If you're not demanding answers but crying out to God for answers that only He can provide, then you're experiencing a normal, healthy relationship with God.

You see, faith and doubt can coexist. We see an example of this in the Gospel of Mark. The father of a demon-possessed boy came to Jesus and begged Him to spare his son's life.

Yet the father's request revealed both faith and doubt. In Mark 9:22, the desperate father said to Jesus, "If You can do anything, take pity on us and help us!" Jesus responded, "'If You can?' All things are possible to him who believes" (v. 23). Then the father confessed his struggle with doubt: "I do believe; help my unbelief" (v. 24). That was good enough. The fact that the father came to Jesus was an act of faith. Jesus healed his boy (vv. 25–27).

The apostle Peter knew that when life doesn't work out the way we want, we become susceptible to the enemy's lies. That's why he said in 1 Peter 5:8–9, "Be of sober spirit, be on the alert. Your adversary, the devil, prowls around like a roaring lion, seeking someone to devour. But resist him, firm in your faith, knowing that the same experiences of suffering are being accomplished by your brethren who are in the world."

When we go through times of suffering, Satan taunts us with questions and accusations against God:

- "Where is God now that you need Him?"
- "Why has God singled you out for pain and heartbreak?"
- "Why isn't God listening to your prayers? He must have forgotten about you."
- "Why does God bless others and not you?"
- "Maybe God really doesn't love you."

During difficult times, these types of questions often sow seeds of doubt. If we're not careful, we will water these seeds and come to believe that God is neither good nor loving.

Satan knows that if our doubts grow, then we'll begin to question the character and power of God, and we'll no longer go to Him for help.

One of my favorite hymns of the faith is "It Is Well with My Soul." You may be familiar with the song, but you may not know the story behind it. The lyrics were penned by Horatio Spafford, a successful Chicago lawyer and real estate investor. In 1871, Horatio's business went up in flames during the Great Chicago Fire, and he spent the next two years rebuilding it. In 1873, he and his wife, Anna, decided a trip to Europe would be a welcome respite for them and their four girls. However, a last-minute business emergency prevented him from accompanying his family across the Atlantic. He decided to take a later ship and meet them in England.

Four days into the Atlantic crossing, the ship Anna and their girls were on collided with another ship and sank. All four of their daughters were lost at sea. When Anna reached Wales she telegraphed Horatio: "Saved alone. What shall I do . . ."[2]

Such terrible loss could have hardened Horatio's and Anna's hearts toward God. But it didn't. Instead, Anna told a minister who survived the shipwreck, "God gave me four daughters. Now they have been taken from me. Someday I will understand why."[3] That's faith in action.

Horatio immediately booked passage from New York to be with his wife. When the ship reached the area of the tragedy, the captain notified Horatio that they were passing over the spot where his daughters had perished. Horatio returned to his cabin and penned the words that have comforted many grieving hearts:

When peace, like a river, attendeth my way,
When sorrow like sea billows roll;
Whatever my lot, Thou has taught me to say,
It is well, it is well with my soul.[4]

Horatio and Anna Spafford had times of deep doubt, but they never surrendered to unbelief. Doubt is a process we all go through to strengthen our faith. Doubters honestly search for truth; unbelievers actively run from truth. Doubters look for reasons to believe; unbelievers look for reasons not to believe. Doubters ask questions; unbelievers refuse answers. God accepts doubters; He rejects unbelievers.

Reasons for Doubt

Christian writer Frederick Buechner had a humorous perspective on the relationship between doubt and faith. He wrote, "Doubts are the ants in the pants of faith. They keep it awake and moving."[5] Let's consider four of these "ants" that can cause us to doubt.

Unlived Truth

My friend and mentor Howard Hendricks used to say, "Nothing will create more doubt in your lives than trafficking in unlived truth." When there is a disconnect between what we believe and what we do, it doesn't take long for doubt to creep into our thinking. The dissonance between belief and behavior, especially if it persists, always brings doubt. You cannot talk like the pious and walk like the pagan for long. Let me tell you what's going to happen; I've seen it too many times. You're eventually going to give up that behavior, or you're going to give up your belief in Christ. A Christian cannot hold on to both of those things for a long period of time.

Unexamined Faith

A lot of Christians live by the adage "The Bible says it; I believe it; that settles it." But this isn't a wise way to live. Eventually, your beliefs will come under attack, perhaps from a movie you watch, an interview you listen to, a class you take, a book you read, or a child you raise. If you have never examined the faith for yourself—to understand why you believe what you believe—you run the risk of wrestling with doubts. It is not enough to believe; you must know *why* you believe.

Unanswered Prayer

Nothing causes us to doubt God's goodness, wisdom, and existence more than when we ask for His help only to hear silence from heaven. Perhaps you have a legitimate need and have begged God to intervene, yet you're convinced your prayers never go beyond the ceiling.

The prophet Daniel knew something of that kind of doubt. God chose to reveal mysteries about the future of Israel to Daniel. One of those mysteries involved "great conflict" (Dan. 10:1). Troubled by the revelation, Daniel prayed for twenty-one days but received no answer . . . until an unexpected visitor arrived (vv. 4–9). The angel who came to him said, "Do not be afraid, Daniel, for from the first day that you set your heart on understanding this and on humbling yourself before your God, your words were heard, and I have come in response to your words" (v. 12). Why did it take three weeks for the angel to get from God's throne room to Daniel's bedroom? The angel explained, "I was waylaid by the angel-prince of the kingdom of Persia and was delayed for a good three weeks. But then Michael, one of the chief angel-princes, intervened to help me" (v. 13 MSG). While it's hard to say how common a scenario like this is, sometimes demonic forces can delay our answers to prayer.

But this is only one of the reasons our prayers may be delayed. Another possibility for unanswered prayer is unconfessed sin. In Isaiah 59:2, the Lord said, "Your iniquities have made a separation between you and your God, and your sins have hidden His face from you so that He does not hear."

Other times, God does not answer our prayers because of idolatry. In Ezekiel 14:3, God told Ezekiel, "These men have set up their idols in their hearts and have put right before their faces the stumbling block of their iniquity. Should I be consulted by them at all?"

Another possibility for unanswered prayer is a lack of generosity. Malachi 3:8 is clear that if we don't give God the offering that belongs to Him, then we're robbing God. The Lord says those who rob Him are cursed, but those who give open themselves to His blessings (vv. 9–10).

Sometimes unanswered prayers are the sovereign will of God. For example, in Romans 1:13, the apostle Paul wanted to go to Rome, but God had a different plan. He wanted Paul to preach the gospel where it had never been preached before.

If you're struggling with doubts because of unanswered prayer, I encourage you to examine your heart and motives, then trust that God will answer in His perfect time.

Undeserved Suffering

If you ask the average person, "What question would you like to ask God?" he or she will likely respond with this: "Why does God allow evil and suffering?" If we're honest, most of us have wondered about that. And of course, often what we're really asking is, "Why does God allow bad things to happen to *me*?"

The problem of undeserved suffering threw theologian Bart Ehrman's faith into doubt. Unable to find answers that satisfied him, Ehrman allowed his doubt to turn to unbelief. In his book *God's Problem: How the Bible Fails to Answer Our Most Important Question—Why We Suffer*, Ehrman wrote, "Suffering is not only senseless, it is also random, capricious, and unevenly distributed."[6]

After the death of his wife, theologian C. S. Lewis also wrestled with doubt. In his book *A Grief Observed*, Lewis wrote, "The conclusion I dread is not 'So there's no God after all,' but 'So this is what God's really like. Deceive yourself no longer.'"[7] This is what suffering can do to our faith.

Dissecting a Doubter

What causes a person to doubt? To see what makes a frog jump, you dissect it. The same could be said for what makes a doubter doubt, and the perfect specimen for such an experiment is the disciple Thomas.

Thomas is presented in the Gospels as a champion doubter. Because Thomas admitted his doubts, we tend to look down on him. But I like Thomas. He was honest and forthright. He didn't pretend to accept things just so he could fit in with the crowd. Thomas was an independent thinker. He wasn't afraid to raise his hand and press for answers he hadn't quite grasped.

I find that refreshing because Thomas was brave enough to voice what the rest of us think but are too afraid to admit. He's a spiritual everyman—a stand-in for our own confusion. There are times in all our lives when we wrestle with doubt. How much better would we be if we were more like Thomas, openly asking our questions and admitting our doubts rather than denying them? When we're willing to put our doubts to the test, especially about life, the future, and God, we can grow in our faith.

Doubts about Life

John 11 is the first record in the Bible of Thomas saying anything. Most of us are familiar with this passage because of what Jesus did later in the chapter: He raised Lazarus from the dead and declared, "I am the resurrection and the life; he who believes in Me will live even if he dies, and everyone who lives and believes in Me will never die" (vv. 25–26). What Thomas said a few verses earlier is easily forgotten, which is unfortunate because, though it expresses doubt, it was nonetheless courageous and loyal to Christ.

Lazarus and his sisters, Mary and Martha, lived in the village of Bethany, about two miles east of Jerusalem. They were Jesus's friends. And because they were His friends, Mary and Martha thought Jesus would come as soon as He heard about Lazarus's life-threatening illness. But Jesus didn't come immediately. In fact, though Jesus loved this family, He waited two days before making the trek to Bethany (vv. 5–7). He explained why in verse 4: "This sickness is not to end in death, but for the glory of God, so that the Son of

God may be glorified by it." What Jesus meant, of course, was that He would demonstrate His power over death by bringing Lazarus back to life—as a result, God and the Son would receive glory as sovereign over life and death.

The disciples weren't sure about Jesus's plan to travel so close to Jerusalem. After all, the last time Jesus was in Jerusalem, the Jewish leaders tried to stone Him (v. 8). The disciples didn't understand that Jesus was under the protection of the Father until His appointed hour (vv. 9–10).

The disciples also misunderstood what Jesus said about Lazarus being "asleep" (v. 11). Thinking Jesus was talking about Lazarus catching a nap—and not being dead—the disciples reminded Jesus that Lazarus would recover (v. 12). Jesus must have shaken His head and thought, *Knuckleheads!* He clarified, "Lazarus is dead . . . let us go to him" (vv. 14–15).

Thomas had serious doubts that a journey to Jerusalem, or anywhere near there, would end well. He was convinced it would probably mean Jesus's death. But Jesus had laid down the gauntlet: anyone who wished to be His disciple "must deny himself, and take up his cross daily and follow" Him— even if that meant to certain death (Luke 9:23). Thomas may have had doubts, but he also had a stout heart. He said to the other disciples, "Let us also go, so that we may die with Him" (John 11:16).

Doubts about the Future

I'm sure Thomas was just as surprised that he walked out of the village of Bethany without a scratch as he was seeing Lazarus walk out of his tomb. Thomas's doubts about traveling safely to Bethany were past, but that didn't ease his doubts about the future.

In John's next portrait of Thomas, he was in the upper room at the Last Supper, listening to Jesus say things during the Passover meal that indicated His final hours were at hand. Jesus talked about going to the Father's house to prepare a place for them and then returning someday to take them to paradise—and they shouldn't be troubled about this. "You know the way where I am going," Jesus said (John 14:4).

He had barely gotten the words out of His mouth when Thomas blurted out, "Lord, we do not know where You are going, how do we know the way?" (v. 5). Thomas wasn't arguing with Jesus. He was voicing his sincere doubts. Thomas didn't have a clue where Jesus was going, and neither did the other disciples. Where exactly was "the Father's house"? Without a clear understanding of the destination, how could they be sure of the route? That's why Thomas asked, "How do we know the way?"

Let's be honest with ourselves for a moment. All of us have thought at one time or another, *Following Jesus would be a lot easier if I just knew for sure how things would turn out!* Unfortunately, God doesn't operate that way, which is why we're commanded to "walk by faith, not by sight" (2 Cor. 5:7).

Thomas struggled to make the transition from sight to faith—as we all do—so Jesus helped him out. He said, "I am the way, and the truth, and the life; no one comes to the Father but through Me" (John 14:6). It's possible that without Thomas's question, Jesus may not have uttered these words, which have brought hope and comfort to believers for millennia. So let's not be too hard on Thomas. He asked a good question, and it elicited an even better answer.

Of course, Jesus's answer didn't resolve all of Thomas's questions and doubts. How could Jesus be "the way" when they had come to the end of their journey with Him? How could Jesus be "the truth" when there was so much they didn't understand? How could Jesus be "the life" when His death was only hours away? More questions, more doubts—and more opportunities for faith.

Doubts about God

For three days after Jesus's crucifixion, the disciples went into hiding, afraid that the Jewish authorities would come for them next. For three days, holed up in their hiding place, they were plagued by grief and doubt about Jesus. Then the risen Lord appeared to them, turning their sorrow into joy, their fear into courage, and their doubts into conviction.

The disciples were gathered in the same upper room when Jesus suddenly stood in their midst and greeted them (John 20:19). He showed them the scars in His hands, in His side, and in His feet, and He empowered them with the Holy Spirit. Then He commissioned them to be His witnesses to the world (vv. 20–23). As you could imagine, the disciples were overjoyed to see Jesus alive!

Then John offered this ominous note: "But Thomas, one of the twelve, . . . was not with them when Jesus came" (v. 24). In John's third picture of the doubting disciple, Thomas was AWOL. Where was Thomas? Why wasn't he with the other disciples in the upper room? We don't know, but apparently the other disciples tracked him down and "were saying to him"—the imperfect tense means they kept at Thomas—"We have seen the Lord!" (v. 25). The disciples told Thomas that Jesus appeared to them not as a ghost but alive and in the flesh. But Thomas would have none of it. He knew all about Roman crucifixion. He had seen Jesus die with his own eyes. He insisted, "Unless I see in His hands the imprint of the nails, and put my finger into the place of the nails, and put my hand into His side, I will not believe" (v. 25).

Consumed by sorrow and doubt, Thomas made the mistake of isolating himself from other believers. When it comes to moving the mountain of doubt, there's an important lesson here: *distance from others is dangerous for doubters.* Lone Rangers are easily ambushed. In our society, it's easy to isolate ourselves behind our smartphones and tablets. But it can be risky for our faith, especially if we're wrestling with unresolved questions. Faith is strengthened in community; doubt is strengthened in isolation. When we struggle with doubts, it is tempting to pull away from other believers. Don't. That is just the time when we need to lean into the fellowship of faith.

Of course, we can't leave Thomas wallowing in his doubts about faith. And fortunately for Thomas, neither could Jesus.

Thomas asked for proof, which the disciples couldn't give. But instead of leaving them again, this time Thomas stayed with the other disciples, who were confident in their faith because they had seen the resurrected Lord. Thomas had to endure an entire week of distressing doubts, but at least he wasn't alone. Notice that the disciples welcomed Thomas, even though he was a doubter. The church should be a place where doubters can find fellowship among those who don't doubt.

Eight days later, the disciples, including Thomas, were in their hideout when "Jesus . . . stood in their midst and said, 'Peace be with you'" (v. 26). Turning to Thomas, Jesus stretched out His hands and said, "Put your finger here." Then He said, "Reach out your hand and put it into my side." The Lord said to Thomas, "Stop doubting and believe" (v. 27 NIV). Isn't that just like Jesus? He didn't treat Thomas with scorn and judgment but with gentleness and grace. Can you imagine what we could achieve for Christ if we—the church—followed in His footsteps when it came to dealing with doubters?

There is a second lesson for us to learn here: *dependable evidence is distributed to doubters.* This is especially true for those who doubt the deity and resurrection of Jesus Christ. Agnostic Josh McDowell and investigative journalist Lee Strobel both set out to debunk the notion of Jesus's resurrection, but after investigating the evidence, both came to believe in the biblical and historical account of the resurrection.[8] If you need answers to your questions and assurance to relieve your doubts, Jesus has what you need.

In the presence of the living Lord, all Thomas's question marks were suddenly straightened into exclamation marks. "My Lord and my God!" he cried (v. 28). No one had addressed Jesus like this before. Thomas's doubts took a sudden leap forward into faith. His doubts weren't irrational, and his questions weren't skeptical. He was honestly searching for the truth.

Then Jesus said, "Because you have seen Me, have you believed? Blessed are they who did not see, and yet believed" (v. 29). That brings us to the third lesson from this passage: *dearly treasured are those who are doubtless.* To those of us who set aside our doubts and follow Christ in faith, though we've never physically seen His face or heard His voice, Jesus pronounces us blessed—favored by God. This is the reward for declaring Jesus as our Lord and our God.

The Path from Doubt to Faith

There's no greater reward for believers than to hear Jesus say to us, "Well done, good and faithful servant" (Matt. 25:21, 23 NIV). If we want to receive this praise from Christ, we must learn to deal with our doubts. I believe there are at least three practical things we should do if we're to be more like Thomas, transforming our doubts into faith.[9]

Don't Deny Your Doubts; Acknowledge Them

When it comes to dealing with your doubts, honesty is the best policy—and it starts with being honest with yourself. The first thing to do when you experience doubt is this: *don't deny your doubts; acknowledge them.*

Many people are afraid to admit they don't have all the answers. Why don't we want to admit our doubts? Deep down, we're afraid that our questions are greater than God's answers. We think the truth of Christianity may be weaker than the lies of atheism—that somehow, someday Christianity will be exposed as fraudulent. Can I tell you something? God can take all comers.

Late in the nineteenth century, German philosopher Friedrich Nietzsche famously declared, "God is dead." Today, God declares, "Nietzsche is dead." Philosophers come and go, but Jesus Christ remains. Trendy theories come and go, but biblical truth remains. As Isaiah 40:8 says, "The grass withers, the flower fades, but the word of our God stands forever."

God is never disappointed or threatened by candid questions. He's big enough to handle our doubts. Years ago, I was talking with a Christian who was questioning her faith. With tears in her eyes, she said, "I'm not sure I believe in God anymore." I said, "That's okay. Even when you don't believe in Him, He still believes in you."

Don't Dread Your Doubts; Analyze Them

We tend to dread our doubts because we fear what our doubts will mean to our faith if we acknowledge them, and we also fear what others would think if our doubts were known. The problem with cowering in fear and refusing to acknowledge your doubts is that they'll catch up with you in the end. When days grow difficult, you won't have the faith to sustain you. This brings us to the second practical application: *don't dread your doubts; analyze them.*

What caused you to doubt? Was it something someone said, maybe a so-called expert you saw on television, or an article you read? Maybe you're the type of person who wants to have all the answers, with no mysteries in the universe. Is that the reason? Were you hurt by a spiritual leader? Did your supposedly godly spouse have an affair? Did God disappoint you in some way? Did He not answer a prayer or come through when you thought He should have?

Whatever the reason for your doubts, face them squarely and name them clearly. There's nothing to dread. There's no question or concern that God hasn't heard or dealt with before. And if it helps, there's a good chance that the doubt you're struggling with is the same doubt others are struggling with too. Remember, Thomas had the courage to say what the other disciples were thinking but were too afraid to say.

Don't Disguise Your Doubts; Articulate Them

Refusing to talk about your doubts is also rooted in fear. But if you can acknowledge them and analyze them, then you can share them. That brings us to the third practical step in this process: *don't disguise your doubts; articulate them.*

When doubts begin to grow, we can nip them in the bud if we expose them to the light by sharing them with a mature believer. My mentor and seminary professor Howard Hendricks often told his students that everyone needs a Paul as a mentor and a Barnabas as a friend. As Solomon pointed out in Ecclesiastes 4:9–12, "Two are better than one because they have a good return for their labor; for if either of them falls, the one will lift up his companion. But woe to the one who falls when there is not another to lift him up! Furthermore, if two lie down together they keep warm, but how can one be warm alone? And if one can overpower him who is alone, two can resist him. A cord of three strands is not quickly torn apart."

Don't talk about your doubts only with other believers; talk about them with the Lord too. I like author Mark Littleton's simple formula for dealing with doubt: "Turn your doubts to questions. Turn your questions to prayers. Turn your prayers to God."[10]

When we turn to God and ask Him our questions, He shows up and encourages us, as He did with Thomas: "Do not be unbelieving, but believing" (John 20:27).

A Steadfast Heart Full of Faith

Thomas never forgot those words. According to tradition, he went to India and then to China, where he established a church in Peking. Returning to India, Thomas converted thousands to Christ and established churches throughout the land. As an old man, Thomas was in a cave praying when

Brahman priests, fearing Christianity would overtake Hinduism, thrust him through with a spear. The apostle dragged himself to a nearby chapel, held on to a stone cross, and prayed, "Lord, I thank Thee for all Thy mercies. Into Thy hands I commend my spirit."[11]

Those are not the dying words of a doubter but of a person with a steadfast heart full of faith. And one day, when you've conquered the mountain of doubt, they can be your dying words as well.

TWO

MOVING FROM
GUILT TO REPENTANCE

THE INTERNAL REVENUE SERVICE has a special fund called the "cheater's account." That way, people who feel guilty about cheating on their taxes can send money anonymously. I read that the IRS supposedly received an anonymous envelope with a money order for $10,000 and this note:

> I've been cheating on my taxes for years, and I feel so guilty I can't sleep at night. Enclosed please find a money order for $10,000.
>   P.S. If I still can't sleep, I'll send in the rest of what I owe.[1]

Proverbs 28:1 says, "The wicked flee when no one is pursuing." Everywhere we look, we see people trying to run away from their consciences—the girl who had an abortion and is afraid to tell her parents; the husband who is involved in a secret liaison and is afraid to tell his wife; the young woman who wrestles with same-sex attraction and is afraid to tell her church leaders; the businessperson who is wasting time at work and is afraid to tell his boss; the student who uses illegal drugs and is afraid to tell her teacher. The list goes on and on.

Guilt is like an acid that eats away our conscience—drip by drip. It's something we can never outrun, but we can stop the drip. Everyone at one time or another faces the mountain of guilt. We can choose to ignore it, or we can repent and enjoy the freedom of a clear conscience. In this chapter we'll look at how to do that, but before we do, we need to come to grips with the reality of guilt.

The Contour of Guilt

Guilt is a mountain that blocks our path to repentance and a clear conscience. And according to the Bible, it has a certain contour and shape.

Two Types of Guilt

All of us stand guilty before God's judgment before we come to faith in Christ. Theologians call this *judicial guilt*. As the One who established the rules of good and evil, God has the right to judge all who violate His standards. We might have our opinions about what is moral and immoral, but God operates on a different level. He doesn't submit His ethical standards to opinion polls, and He doesn't judge based on our standards. And His benchmark is nothing less than perfection. "Be holy, because I am holy," is God's measuring stick (1 Pet. 1:16 NIV). Paul made it clear that none of us measures up: "All have sinned and fall short of the glory of God" (Rom. 3:23).

One sin is all it takes to be declared guilty by God. That's the bad news. Fortunately, the Bible offers good news. Our judicial guilt will be removed if we put our faith in the death and resurrection of Jesus Christ as the *only* means of standing guiltless before God. We accept, in faith, that God "made Him who knew no sin to be sin on our behalf, so that we might become the righteousness of God in Him" (2 Cor. 5:21). When we put our faith in Jesus Christ, our judicial guilt is removed immediately. We're declared righteous. As Paul said, "There is now no condemnation for those who are in Christ Jesus" (Rom. 8:1). We go from guilty to not guilty by believing in Jesus.

Yet believers continue to sin as long as we are in this fallen world. And when we sin, we suffer the second type of guilt, called *ethical guilt*. The Bible refers to this as the Holy Spirit convicting us of sin (John 16:8). In other words, He slaps us upside our spiritual heads.

Christians sometimes confuse the Holy Spirit's conviction, which is true guilt, with other convictions—false guilt. The difference between the two has to do with whose yardstick is being used to measure right and wrong. False guilt comes when we violate temporal standards set by ourselves, others, or society. For example, a perfectionist may feel false guilt when he doesn't measure up to his own standards. A single mother may feel guilty when her home doesn't look like the cover of *Southern Living*. Or a young Christian couple may feel guilty when they kiss before marriage.

True guilt, on the other hand, comes from violating the standards set by God, as expressed in His Word. When Christians knowingly and willfully disobey God's Word, we usually feel true guilt. We feel that way because we *are* guilty.

Two Responses to Guilt

Psalm 32 is called a *maskl*, which in Hebrew means "instruction." Whenever we come across one of these *maskl* psalms, we're meant to learn something. In Psalm 32, we're to learn about responding to guilt.

The first response is *silence*. David put it like this: "When I kept silent about my sin, my body wasted away through my groaning all day long" (v. 3). Silence and secrecy are natural responses to those facing the mountain of guilt. Guilt forces us into isolation. We hide, running away to a place where we think no one can find out about our sin.

When my daughters were younger and did something they knew was wrong, their first reaction was to hide the evidence and promise each other to keep the secret. To show how serious they were, they would pretend to lock their mouths with a key, saying, "Cross my heart and hope to die, stick a needle in my eye." But the longer they remained silent, the more the Holy Spirit needled their consciences, until they couldn't stand it any longer and finally confessed.

The second response to guilt is *sorrow*. David wrote, "For day and night Your hand was heavy upon me; my vitality was drained away as with the fever heat of summer" (v. 4). In earlier times, David would have said, "It's good to be king." Palace servants catered to his every whim, army generals jumped when he commanded, and the people celebrated his every action. Yet David was a prisoner to his own tortured conscience. Overcome with guilt, he felt the very essence of life draining from him, like water running down the street instead of being absorbed into the soil and giving life. And so it goes. Guilt is accompanied by sorrow and, if not dealt with, can bring tragic consequences, as David's life will attest.

The Case of a Guilty Man

By any standard David was one of the greatest men ever to have lived. He had the heart of a poet, the soul of a priest, the mind of a philosopher, and the body of a warrior. He spent his early years tending sheep, protecting them from predators. He became famous as a giant-killer. After he was anointed as Israel's future king, David served as Saul's understudy and spent years running from a jealous king intent on murder. With the nation finally unified under his powerful hand, David was finally king of the mountain, and nothing could knock him off the summit. He had everything he ever wanted. He was the king of God's people, Israel. He was the Lord's anointed.

And he was bored.

David had conquered lions and bears, giants and armies. But now he faced an enemy that sent shivers down his spine: the ennui that comes with midlife. While Israel's army was off fighting (2 Sam. 11:1), David looked for a new mountain to conquer. He found one that fell on him like a rockslide.

You likely know the story. David was walking on the roof of his palace and saw a beautiful woman bathing (v. 2). Since indoor plumbing didn't exist at the time, it wasn't unusual for people to take care of necessary hygiene outside. In all likelihood, the woman was in her private courtyard.

But David couldn't take his eyes off her. He called a servant to ask who she was. "Is this not Bathsheba, the daughter of Eliam, the wife of Uriah the Hittite?" the servant said (v. 3). This is an interesting question, since Eliam was one of David's mighty men (23:34), whose father was one of David's advisers.[2] And Uriah served as a member of the king's elite fighting force. Suspecting what might be going through David's mind, the servant in essence was saying to the king, "Hey, just so you know, Bathsheba is married to Uriah, one of your best soldiers. And her father is Eliam, another of your elite warriors."[3] In other words, "David, whatever you're thinking about Bathsheba, put it out of your mind. She's off-limits. Think about the people you'd hurt."

But the servant's warning fell on deaf ears. It's like Tony in the movie *West Side Story*. When he first sees Maria at the dance, even though he knows Maria's brother is the leader of a rival gang, all Tony can think about is Maria. The movie depicts this by distorting everyone around them while shining a spotlight on Maria. That's how I imagine it was for David when he saw Bathsheba.

The king "sent messengers and took her" back to the palace, where David had his way with her (11:4). Soon afterward, she informed David, "I am pregnant" (v. 5).

How did David respond to the news? He summoned Bathsheba's husband, Uriah, from the battlefield and tried to trick him into sleeping with his wife (vv. 6–8). But Uriah refused to return to his house, reasoning, "The Ark and the armies of Israel and Judah are living in tents, and Joab and my master's men are camping in the open fields. How could I go home to wine and dine and sleep with my wife?" (v. 11 NLT). David then hatched the plan that made him a murderer: "The next morning David wrote a letter to Joab [the commander of his forces] and gave it to Uriah to deliver. The letter instructed Joab, 'Station Uriah on the front lines where the battle is fiercest. Then pull back so that he will be killed'" (vv. 14–15 NLT).

Joab obeyed the order, and Uriah was killed. Then David married Bathsheba. But "the thing that David had done was evil in the sight of the LORD" (v. 27).

The Consequences for a Guilty Man

That is a chilling indictment against David: "the thing . . . was evil in the sight of the LORD." Yet the Lord didn't punish David—not immediately. Days and weeks and months passed without any visible judgment from God. Initially, David must have thought he had dodged a divine arrow. He came to the same conclusion we often draw when God delays His discipline: we mistakenly interpret God's mercy as His tolerance of sin. Ironically, it was David's and Bathsheba's second son, Solomon, who wrote about this in Ecclesiastes: "Because the sentence against an evil deed is not executed quickly, therefore the hearts of the sons of men among them are given fully to do evil" (8:11).

However, it's a mistake to believe that just because God doesn't settle His accounts immediately, He never settles them. The apostle Paul warned, "Do not be deceived, God is not mocked; for whatever a man sows, this he will also reap" (Gal. 6:7).

Although there were no external signs of God's judgment for at least nine months after David's sins, God was dealing with the king internally. David lived under a mountain of guilt that crushed the life out of him physically, emotionally, and spiritually. He referred to this in Psalm 32, saying, "When I kept silent about my sin, my body wasted away through my groaning all day long. For day and night Your hand was heavy upon me; my vitality was drained away as with the fever heat of summer" (vv. 3–4).

The Physical Consequences of Guilt: Grinding

When David said his "body wasted away" because of his secret sin, he was referring to his bones or joints causing severe pain throughout his body. And when he said, "My vitality was drained away as with the fever heat of summer," he meant that his strength was sapped as if he had a fever of 103 degrees. Though usually a robust man even in midlife, David now creaked around without even the strength to get out of bed. Today, we would say he was aging before his time.

The idea that unconfessed sin leads to physical pain is mentioned often in the psalms.[4] Medical science verifies what David and others have written. According to one expert, "The awareness of wrongdoing often produces prolonged feelings of remorse and self-condemnation that, lacking catharsis, can actually have damaging effects on the bodily systems and open the gates to disease."[5] The physical effects of unresolved guilt can range from sluggishness and weight gain to a complete breakdown of the immune system.

When I think of the physical effects of guilt, I recall the story of Robert Ebeling, a space shuttle engineer who knew that the O-rings designed to seal the joints between the booster rocket's segments became brittle in cold temperatures. With the *Challenger* sitting on the pad the day before launch, Florida experienced a severe cold snap. Ebeling and other engineers passionately argued with NASA officials that the launch should be postponed. Their pleas fell on deaf ears. On January 28, 1986, Ebeling watched in horror as the *Challenger* exploded, killing all seven crew members. Ebeling never forgave himself for failing to halt that launch. He said, "I've been under terrible stress since the accident. I have headaches. I cry. I have bad dreams. I go into a hypnotic trance almost daily."[6] That's what unresolved guilt will do to you.

The Emotional Consequences of Guilt: Groaning

There are also emotional consequences of guilt. This is what David alluded to in Psalm 32:3 when he said he was "groaning all day long." Guilt manifests itself emotionally in two ways.

Depression is probably the most common emotional consequence of unresolved guilt. Christian psychiatrists Frank Minirth and Paul Meyer observed that the patients they saw for depression often wrestled with guilt. "They feel guilty because they are guilty," they wrote. "And straightening out the wrong they are doing is sometimes all that is needed to straighten out their feelings of depression."[7]

Anxiety is the other emotional manifestation of guilt. I imagine David lived in constant fear that at some point his secret would be revealed. The fact that he engaged in such an elaborate scheme to cover up his actions proves how much he dreaded being discovered. And, as we will see, his worst nightmare became a reality.

I remember counseling a man who exhibited both depression and anxiety because he refused to repent of his sin. He was remorseful, but that was all. He had been involved in an illicit relationship for years. The woman in the relationship discovered she was pregnant and married another man. The man I was counseling, the father of the baby, explained to me that he carried a disease that threatened the lives of both the mother and the baby. He was deeply depressed over losing his lover and anxious that she and his child might die as a result of his actions. Yet he didn't plan to change anything in his life as a result of this episode. It wasn't suprising then that he remained depressed and anxious.

The Spiritual Consequences of Guilt: Groveling

Finally, there are the spiritual consequences of guilt. Though David didn't use the word, the idea of groveling is found in his admission that the heavy hand of God was upon him "day and night" (Ps. 32:4). It's the picture of being held down, your face in the dirt, while the full body weight of another sits on you. Spiritually, that was David, groveling on the ground.

Unsettled guilt leads to a break in our fellowship with God. It's important to understand that David's position in God's eyes never changed. Sin never changes God's attitude toward true believers. But sin changes *our* attitude toward God. Guilt breaks a relationship between two people, even when only one of the parties feels guilty. Adam and Eve are perfect illustrations of this principle. After their sin, they were so consumed by guilt that they hid from the presence of God, who had come to the garden to have fellowship with them (Gen. 3:8–10).

Unsettled guilt also leads to the discipline of God. God isn't in the business of allowing His sinful children to go unpunished. Hebrews 12:6 makes this clear: "For those whom the Lord loves He disciplines, and He scourges every son whom He receives." That's what happened to David. Through the prophet Nathan, the Lord told David, "The sword shall never depart from your house, because you have despised Me and have taken the wife of Uriah the Hittite to be your wife" (2 Sam. 12:10). God assured David that his sins were forgiven (v. 13). But that didn't mean the consequences of his sin were forgotten. David had to suffer those, and they were severe.

God disciplines His children who continue in sin. The purpose of such discipline is restoration and is evidence of God's love. Recently, a man was in my office detailing the turmoil in his life—his wife had left him, his business had collapsed, and his health was deteriorating. When I asked him about his spiritual life, he admitted that he was living far from God. When I suggested that maybe God was allowing these circumstances so that he might restore his relationship with God, he responded, "I just have one question: Where do I start?" Fortunately, the road to repentance is quite simple.

And that's where we next find David.

The Confession of a Guilty Man

The Lord sent the prophet Nathan to the king with a story about a rich man and a poor man. A guest was staying in the rich man's house, but the rich man didn't want to kill one of his many sheep to feed his guest. Instead, he took the poor man's only lamb, which was like a pet to that family, and prepared it for his guest (2 Sam. 12:1–4). When he heard that, David burned with fury and said, "As the LORD lives, surely the man who has done this deserves to die" (v. 5).

Then, with four simple words, Nathan plunged a figurative dagger into David's heart: "You are the man!" (v. 7).

The Lord had anointed David and made him king over Israel. The Lord had rescued David from the hands of Saul. And the Lord had provided for David companionship, wealth, power, and fame (vv. 7–8). Yet David had "despised the word of the LORD" by taking Uriah's wife and Uriah's life (v. 9).

The jig was up. David's secret was revealed. This was a critical moment for David: he could either deny Nathan's accusations or confess his sin. Fortunately for David (and us), he chose the latter path. "I have sinned against the LORD," he admitted (v. 13).

Contrary to popular opinion, repentance isn't an emotion; it's an attitude that leads to an action. The Greek verb *metanoeo*, which is translated "repent," means a change of mind that leads to a change of direction. It's a spiritual U-turn.

David demonstrated both a changed attitude and changed actions in Psalm 51. The psalm introduction reads, "A Psalm of David, when Nathan the prophet came to him, after he had gone in to Bathsheba." David penned this psalm soon after his fateful confrontation with the prophet.

David said the attitude we must have when confessing our sins to the Lord is "a broken spirit; a broken and a contrite heart." That is the only "sacrifice" the Lord "will not despise" (v. 17). Such spiritual brokenness leads to the conviction that we must turn from our sin. If we do, then we'll find the forgiveness we need. Proverbs 28:13 puts it like this: "He who conceals his transgressions will not prosper, but he who confesses and forsakes them will find compassion." That was the attitude David exhibited when Nathan called him out.

Having the proper attitude, however, is only the beginning. An attitude of brokenness must lead to the actions of confession and repentance.

Acknowledge Your Sin as Sinful

We often try to cope with the mountain of guilt by minimizing our sin or using euphemisms to diminish it. But God calls things as they are.

David used five significant words in Psalm 51 to describe his sin. The first is *transgressions* (vv. 1, 3). This word carries with it moral gravity. When we call a person a "transgressor," it marks them as being a rebel who is revolting against God's standards of right and wrong.

The second word is *iniquity* (vv. 2, 5, 9). This word captures the perversity of our sin nature. Paul said in Romans 3: "There is none righteous, not even one" (v. 10). The idea of looking within ourselves and finding good is not a biblical idea.

Third is the word *sin*, used five times in Psalm 51. This is the universal term for wrong attitudes and actions. It's when we "fall short of the glory of God" (Rom. 3:23) by missing the mark—the target God has set up for our lives, which is holiness. It's going to a gun range and hitting the target next to you, or going bowling and knocking down the pins in the other lane.

The fourth word is *evil* (v. 4). This word indicates seeing wrongdoing from God's perspective. In the eyes of God, all sin is considered evil, something vile and worthy of condemnation.

Finally, there is *bloodguiltiness* (v. 14). This is David's confession of murder—of taking another person's life without divine authorization (as might be in the case of capital punishment or warfare).

David didn't mince words when it came to his sin, and neither should we.

Accept Responsibility for Your Sin

Once you acknowledge that your sin is indeed sinful, the next step is to accept responsibility for your sin. You don't make excuses or blame others for your sin.

I remember reading a *Calvin and Hobbes* cartoon that illustrated our culture of victimhood. Calvin said, "Nothing I do is my fault. My family is dysfunctional, and my parents don't empower me! Consequently, I'm not self-actualized! My behavior is addictive, functioning in a diseased process of toxic codependency! I need holistic healing and wellness before I'll accept any responsibility for my actions! I love the culture of victimhood." Hobbes's response was simple: "One of us needs to stick his head in a bucket of ice water."[8]

David didn't need to stick his head in a bucket of ice water, not after Nathan threw the bucket at him. Throughout Psalms 32 and 51 David used the personal pronouns *I*, *me*, and *mine*. For example, look at the first three verses in Psalm 51: "Be gracious to *me*, O God, according to Your lovingkindness; according to the greatness of Your compassion blot out *my* transgressions. Wash *me* thoroughly from *my* iniquity and cleanse *me* from *my* sin. For *I* know *my* transgressions, and *my* sin is ever before *me*."

There's no scapegoating with this shepherd-king, and there should be none with us. To distance ourselves from guilt, we must first recognize our sin. *We must identify areas*

in our lives where we have fallen short of God's standard.
True repentance requires an honest evaluation of our lives. In
Psalm 139:23–24, David put it like this: "Search me, O God,
and know my heart; try me and know my anxious thoughts;
and see if there be any hurtful way in me [that hurts You], and
lead me in the everlasting way." Here's a checklist of areas
that deserve serious consideration:

- *Your relationship with God.* Do you have any unconfessed sins or any unkept promises?
- *Your relationship with your family.* Do you need
  to make restitution with your parents, siblings, or
  children?
- *Your relationship with your mate.* Do you need to
  ask for forgiveness for wrongs done or said to your
  husband or wife?
- *Your relationship with others.* Do you need to end an
  immoral relationship or seek forgiveness from someone you've offended?
- *Your relationship with yourself.* Do you need to stop
  sinful habits and start godly habits?
- *Your relationship with your possessions.* Do you
  need to transfer your trust in your bank account to
  the Lord?

We must make restitution where necessary. If you've
wronged another person, it's necessary to seek that person's
forgiveness. Jesus said, "If you are presenting your offering at the altar, and there remember that your brother has
something against you, leave your offering there before the

altar and go; first to be reconciled to your brother, and then come and present your offering" (Matt. 5:23–24).

Sometimes monetary restitution might be in order. When the tax collector Zacchaeus, who had robbed others by over-taxing them, came to faith in Christ, he immediately restored what had been defrauded. He told Jesus, "Behold, Lord, half of my possessions I will give to the poor, and if I have defrauded anyone of anything, I will give back four times as much" (Luke 19:8). Such an action is a sign of genuine repentance.

We must also turn away from known sin. It's possible to follow the first two steps without truly repenting. Remember, the word *repent* carries the idea of turning around. When David asked for God's forgiveness, he also asked for some-thing else: a steadfast spirit. He prayed, "Create in me a clean heart, O God, and renew a steadfast spirit within me" (Ps. 51:10). David realized that his previous way of think-ing had led him into his present desperate situation. True repentance necessitates a new game plan for life. David not only identified those areas but also planned to change them. And so must we.

Address Your Confession of Sin to God

Having acknowledged our sin as sinful and having ac-cepted responsibility for our sin, we now come to the actual act of confession. David obviously couldn't ask forgiveness from Uriah, but he could from Bathsheba. He had wronged her deeply. He had manipulated her and made her a widow. Even Joab, the commander of David's army, had been a pawn in David's wicked game, forced to compromise his integrity. And we haven't even talked about the wrong done to the people of Israel because of David's abuse of power. Each one deserved an open confession and petition for forgiveness.

Yet neither Bathsheba nor Joab nor the people could remove David's guilt. They could forgive him personally, but the deeper stain of sin would remain because David's sin, like all sin, was ultimately against God. That's why David confessed his sin to God and why we must do the same. He wrote to the Lord, "Against You, You only, I have sinned and done what is evil in Your sight, so that You are justified when You speak and blameless when You judge" (Ps. 51:4).

Repentance begins and ends with God. We may sin against ourselves and against others, but all sin is against God. And if we come to God with broken and contrite hearts, confessing our sin, "He is faithful and righteous to forgive us our sins and to cleanse us from all unrighteousness" (1 John 1:9). And this brings us to the good news about guilt: it can and will be removed for those who confess and repent of their sin.

The Path from Guilt to Repentance

When God forgives us, He removes our sin, restores our joy, renews our fellowship, and refocuses our lives. That's why Psalm 51 is such a helpful passage for those struggling with the mountain of guilt. It highlights the path from guilt to repentance, which leads to a life of blessedness and a clear conscience.

God Removes Our Sin

Like a man covered in dirt and grime, David prayed for a divine bath. He prayed, "Wash me thoroughly from my iniquity and cleanse me from my sin. . . . Purify me with hyssop, and I shall be clean; wash me, and I shall be whiter than snow" (Ps. 51:2, 7). And in verse 9, David prayed, "Hide Your face from my sins and blot out all my iniquities." David used three images in asking God to remove his sin: water, hyssop, and the act of blotting.

Scripture has a twofold meaning for cleansing from sin. First, we are cleansed from the *defilement* of sin, which David symbolized with the imagery of being washed with water. This is what Jesus was pointing to when He washed the disciples' feet. Jesus said to Peter, "He who has bathed needs only to wash his feet, but is completely clean" (John 13:10). In other words, Peter had come to faith in Christ and had been forgiven of his sins, but sinners continue to sin—and when we do, our feet, so to speak, get dirty and need washing again.

Second, we are cleaned from the *guilt* of sin, which David described using the image of hyssop. This is based in the Old Testament, when priests used a branch from a hyssop bush to sprinkle animal blood onto the altar as a symbol of sacrificial death. The writer of Hebrews alluded to this image when speaking about the sacrifice of Christ on the cross: "When He had *made purification of sins*, He sat down at the right hand of the Majesty on high" (Heb. 1:3). This is a once-for-all cleansing, accomplished by the death and resurrection of Jesus Christ. We don't have to crucify Jesus every time we sin, but we do have to "wash our feet."

The third image, the act of blotting, points to offenses jotted in a ledger with blood-red ink. Think of it like a criminal's rap sheet. It's a record of all the crimes he or she has been convicted of. David's rap sheet told an ominous story: adultery, rape, abuse of power, and murder. What could

David do to expunge his record? Nothing—except to throw himself on the mercy of the court in hopes that God would redact David's crimes.

And that's exactly what God did. David wrote in Psalm 103:12: "As far as the east is from the west, so far has [God] removed our transgressions from us." Do you know why David used the directions east and west instead of north and south? There are poles to the north and south. If you traveled north and arrived at the North Pole and kept traveling, you would immediately begin going south (and vice versa if you traveled to the South Pole). But there are no poles east and west. You can travel in one of those directions and never begin traveling in the opposite direction. God does not remove our sin as far as north is from the south, destinations that are marked on a map with an end point, but as far as the east is from the west—namely, to infinity. And that should bring comfort to any forgiven sinner.

God Reinstates Our Joy

God not only removes our sin, but He also reinstates our joy. David prayed, "Make me to hear joy and gladness, let the bones which You have broken rejoice. . . . Restore to me the joy of Your salvation and sustain me with a willing spirit" (Ps. 51:8, 12).

Almost every Christian who comes to my office feeling guilty over some sin admits that the one thing they miss most of all is a sense of joy. They tell me, particularly those who haven't given up their sins, that they are irritable, are miserable, and have a short fuse. That was David to a T.

Though David didn't lose his salvation (which the Bible assures us can never be lost once given), he did lose the joy of his salvation. And the loss of his joy, which came from an unclean conscience, pained him as much as the physical consequences of his guilt. David pleaded for God to restore his broken joy—to set it like a doctor might set a broken bone so it can heal—as he lived a Spirit-filled life where his conscience was clear of sin and guilt.

God Revives Our Fellowship

With the restoration of joy comes the reviving of fellowship with God. David prayed, "Do not cast me away from Your presence, and do not take Your Holy Spirit from me" (Ps. 51:11).

In the Old Testament, the Holy Spirit didn't permanently indwell believers but came and left as the Lord willed. On the day David was anointed king, God removed His Spirit from Saul and filled David instead (1 Sam. 16:13–14). Because of his disobedience, Saul was cut loose from the Lord's fellowship.

Believers who fall into sin today don't have to worry about losing the Holy Spirit. Jesus made that clear in John 10:28–29. But our sin creates a barrier between God and us (Isa. 59:2). The only thing that can break down that barrier and renew our unfettered fellowship with God is repentance. And when we repent, comfort comes to our souls.

God Redeploys Our Lives

The last comfort from guilt mentioned in Psalm 51 is a redeployment into the blessed life. David asked the Lord for "a steadfast spirit" and "a willing spirit" (vv. 10, 12). David was asking God to refocus his life on what was pleasing to Him. David's natural tendency, as well as ours, is to fulfill whatever is pleasing to us. But more times than not, what pleases us leads to sin and guilt. What pleases the Lord always leads to holiness and blessedness. David didn't want to repeat the same tragic mistakes, so he asked God to give him a spirit that would be able to walk the line.

Have you ever prayed for that kind of spirit? You should. In Psalm 32, which also deals with David's sin with Bathsheba, he wrote, "How blessed is he whose transgression is forgiven, whose sin is covered! How blessed is the man to whom the LORD does not impute iniquity, and in whose spirit there is no deceit!" (vv. 1–2).

The word *blessed* means *happy*. If you want to be blessed—to live a happy life—then I urge you to conquer your mountain of guilt by repenting of your sin. As British preacher Charles Spurgeon wrote, "When we deal seriously with our sin, God will deal gently with us. When we hate what the Lord hates, He will soon make an end of it, to our joy and peace."[9]

THREE

MOVING FROM ANXIETY TO PEACE

WHEN NOVELIST F. SCOTT FITZGERALD sent his eleven-year-old daughter away to summer camp in August 1933, he wrote her a brief letter containing a list of things she should worry about and things she shouldn't worry about. The things Fitzgerald advised his daughter to worry about included courage, cleanliness, and horsemanship. The things he told her not to worry about caused me to chuckle because they are things my girls worry about: mosquitoes and flies. And then, like every father speaking to his daughter, he told her, "Don't worry about boys."[1]

Reading Fitzgerald's list might cause us to smile and think, *If all I had to worry about were bugs and boys, my life would be easy!* But of course, there are many things in this world more worrisome than those—and when we worry about them we aren't living life to its fullest, despite its uncertainties, disappointments, and heartaches. This is what Corrie ten Boom, who courageously saved Jews from the Nazis and suffered in a concentration camp after she and her family were found out, was getting at when she wrote, "Worry does not empty tomorrow of sorrow; it empties today of strength."[2]

Most of us know that worrying doesn't change anything, yet we do it all the time. Like Linus from the cartoon *Peanuts*, we carry around our anxieties, our worries, and our fears like a blanket, believing there is security in them.

So, what can we do about our anxious thoughts? I have good news for you: the Word of God has an answer.

The Antecedent to Anxiety

Before we delve into the Scripture, it's worth noting that the mountain of anxiety blocks us from peace. It's my hope that by the time you finish this chapter you'll rediscover the path to peace—the kind that "surpasses all comprehension" (Phil. 4:7). Now, let's look at some important particulars about anxiety.

The Vocabulary of Anxiety

Three times in His famous Sermon on the Mount, Jesus told His audience, "Do not worry" (Matt. 6:25, 31, 34). The apostle Paul picked up this theme when he encouraged believers, "Be anxious for nothing" (Phil. 4:6). Of course that's easier said than done! But for now, let's get a handle on these two words: *worry* and *anxious*.

The Greek word Jesus used for "worry" is *merimno*. Paul used the same Greek word in his letter to the Philippians.

The word means "to be (unduly) concerned"—an excessive concern about things, often about things that are out of our control.[3]

In Latin, the Greek is translated *anixus*, from which we get our word *anxious*. And in German, the word is *wurgen*, from which we get our word *worry*. The idea behind both of these translations is choking or strangling. Jesus used a similar word in Mark 4:7—*sumpnigo*—when He told the parable of the farmer sowing his seed on various soils. The seed that fell among thorns was *choked out*, Jesus said, "and it yielded no crop" (v. 7). Jesus explained why: "These are the ones who have heard the word, but the *worries* [*merimno*] of the world, and the deceitfulness of riches, and the desires for other things enter in and *choke* [*sumpnigo*] the word, and it becomes unfruitful" (vv. 18–19). Anxiety sprouts like a weed and strangles the truth of God's Word, choking out a life of peace.

The Reasons for Anxiety

Where does anxiety come from? There are at least three reasons for anxiety. First, we become anxious because of a *misguided perspective*. Jesus said, "Do not store up for yourselves treasures on earth, where moth and rust destroy, and where thieves break in and steal. But store up for yourselves treasures in heaven, where neither moth nor rust destroys, and where thieves do not break in or steal" (Matt. 6:19–20).

Most anxiety can be traced to fear, which is an emotional alarm to a real or perceived threat. One of our greatest vulnerabilities is the fear of losing something important to us. To conquer that fear, we take action, usually by exhausting ourselves trying to figure out ways to protect our loved ones and ourselves. If we're fearful of poverty, we'll work to accumulate money. If we're fearful about our health, we'll diet, exercise obsessively, and go to the doctor every time we feel an ache or pain. If we're fearful of losing someone's love, we'll smother that person with attention. All these fear-based activities produce anxiety because all of them, in the end, are futile. No matter how hard we try, we cannot protect ourselves against every adversity in life.

We must learn to hold things loosely and see that all we have is a gift from God, and if He so chooses, He has the right to take away those gifts.

Second, we can become anxious as a result of *unconfessed sin*. We saw these verses in the previous chapter, dealing with guilt, but they're applicable here as well: "When I kept silent about my sin, my body wasted away through my groaning all day long. For day and night Your hand was heavy upon me; my vitality was drained away as with the fever heat of summer" (Ps. 32:3–4). Whenever we deliberately violate God's laws, we experience a general sense of uneasiness. That's anxiety. Deep down we know we cannot continue living outside His will, not without the thought that something terrible is going to happen. We fear our sin will be uncovered, and we'll be exposed. Or worse, we fear God is going to "get even" with us.

In time, not only will we feel the ill effects of unconfessed sin, as we saw in chapter 2, but our anxious thoughts will eat a hole through our spirits. The great promise of Scripture, however, is that when we confess our sins, then God will forgive us of our sins (1 John 1:9). With a repaired and renewed spirit, we're ready to accept the nourishment of God's Word; it can flourish within us. Then we can say, as

David did, "When my anxious thoughts multiply within me, Your consolations delight my soul" (Ps. 94:19).

Third, *satanic attack* can also be a basis of anxiety. In Paul's day, soldiers took arrows soaked in tar and ignited them. The only defense against these flaming arrows was a shield covered in waterlogged leather. When the arrows struck the shield, the moisture extinguished the flames. This is why Paul said, "Therefore, take up the full armor of God, so that you will be able to resist in the evil day, and having done everything, to stand firm . . . taking up the shield of faith with which you will be able to extinguish all the flaming arrows of the evil one" (Eph. 6:13, 16).

Satan has many flaming arrows in his arsenal, such as lust, doubt, and materialism—and we'll address many of them in this book. But I think one of Satan's favorite weapons is anxiety. Anxiety causes us to focus on the wrong things. It diverts our attention away from the faithfulness of God and what He's doing in our lives in the present. The past is unchangeable, and the future is unknowable. Yet both can paralyze us with worry.

Satan often uses four little words to strangle the joy and peace out of our lives: "If only" and "What if?" I've talked with men who, years after their divorces, have trouble getting on with their lives because they wish they could win back the hearts of their ex-wives. For many of these men, it's too late. Their ex-wives have already remarried. They confess to me, "If only I had paid more attention to my wife and demonstrated how much I loved her, she wouldn't have left me." Or, "If only I hadn't taken that business trip, or walked into that bar, or began flirting with that coworker, then I wouldn't have had an affair and destroyed my marriage."

Like many parents, I asked a lot of "What if" questions as our daughters were getting older: "What if they don't get into the university they want to attend?" "What if, after graduation, they can't find a job?" "What if they bring home a young man they're serious about but we disapprove of?"

Anxiety also produces distortions about the truth. The devil doesn't want you to know, remember, or apply the truth of God's Word. Jesus called Satan "the father of lies" (John 8:44). Satan invented fake news long before it became a fixture of our cultural and political lexicon.

The Consequences of Anxiety

Anxiety burdens our minds to the point that fear replaces peace, leading to physical and psychological trauma. According to the Anxiety and Depression Association of America, anxiety is a leading cause of mental illness in the United States, affecting forty million adults. Anxiety disorders include panic disorder, social anxiety disorder, obsessive-compulsive disorder, posttraumatic stress disorder, and persistent depressive disorder. Anxiety also can lead to eating disorders, headaches, irritable bowel syndrome, sleep disorders, substance abuse, body dysmorphic disorder, chronic pain, fibromyalgia, and stress.[4] Of course, not all mental disorders are caused by anxiety, but the fact remains that anxiety does have a physical effect on many people.

That's no way to live. And it's not how Jesus wants us to live. We could paraphrase Jesus's promise in John 10:10 like this: "Anxiety comes only to choke out your joy and strangle your peace. But I come to give you life—an invincible life of abundant joy and peace without worry."

Anxiety also strangles our ability to distinguish between what is incidental and what is essential, leading to distractions and distortions. A misguided perspective can lead to anxiety. Conversely, anxiety can lead to a misguided perspective. The endless pursuit of power, position, and possessions is a natural anxiety inducer. We reason that a few sleepless nights and nails chewed to the nub are small prices to pay to achieve these goals, because in our kingdom these are essentials. But in God's kingdom, those things are merely incidentals. Look at what Jesus said in Luke 12:

> Don't fuss about what's on the table at mealtime or if the clothes in your closet are in fashion. There is far more to your inner life than the food you put in your stomach, more to your outer appearance than the clothes you hang on your body. Look at the ravens, free and unfettered, not tied down to a job description, carefree in the care of God. And you count far more.
>
> Has anyone by fussing before the mirror ever gotten taller by so much as an inch? If fussing can't even do that, why fuss at all? Walk into the fields and look at the wildflowers. They don't fuss with their appearance—but have you ever seen color and design quite like it? The ten best-dressed men and women in the country look shabby alongside them. If God gives such attention to the wildflowers, most of them never even seen, don't you think he'll attend to you, take pride in you, do his best for you?
>
> What I'm trying to do here is get you to relax, not be so preoccupied with *getting* so you can respond to God's *giving*. People who don't know God and the way he works fuss over these things, but you know both God and how he works. Steep yourself in God-reality, God-initiative, God-provisions.

You'll find all your everyday human concerns will be met. Don't be afraid of missing out. You're my dearest friends! The Father wants to give you the very kingdom itself. (vv. 22–32 MSG)

Anxiety divides our hearts and displaces God as the center of our lives, leading to conflict with others. This is the old cliché of getting kicked at work and then coming home to kick the dog. Anxiety makes us irritable, and as a result we inevitably take out our irritability on others—usually family members. How many families have been destroyed by adultery, divorce, overbearing parenting, or rebellious children? Each of these is a demonstration of self-centeredness, not God-centeredness.

Such self-centeredness shouldn't be found among believers. But it is. In Romans 12:3, Paul wrote, "For through the grace given to me I say to everyone among you not to think more highly of himself than he ought to think." And in Philippians 2:3, he said, "Do nothing from selfishness or empty conceit, but with humility of mind regard one another as more important than yourselves." In other words, as I used to tell my girls when they were teenagers, "You are a treasure, a pearl of great price, and I love you with a love that knows no bounds. But the world doesn't revolve around you."

God is still on the throne, and He knows what He's doing. Relax. Trust Him. It'll do wonders for your worry.

An Address on Anxiety

Matthew's record of Jesus's sermon on anxiety can be divided into two main sections. In the first, Jesus gives five reasons we shouldn't worry (Matt. 6:25–32); in the second, He gives us one alternative for what we should do instead of worry (vv. 33–34). But before we look at the details of this sermon, a disclaimer or two is in order.

The heart of Jesus's sermon is stated in three simple words: *do not worry* (vv. 25, 31, 34). But that doesn't mean *do not plan*. Many people come to the mistaken conclusion after reading Jesus's sermon that they should live *que sera, sera*: "whatever will be, will be." This attitude gives no serious thought to the future—about the well-being of your family, your career ambitions, or your inheritance. Jesus didn't live that way. Before His death, Jesus trained His disciples to carry on the ministry after His death, resurrection, and ascension. He also taught that it's wise to make sure you have the funds in place before you break ground on your new home or business (Luke 14:28). Failure to plan isn't an act of faith; it's an act of foolishness.

Here's a second disclaimer: Jesus's command not to worry doesn't mean *do not be concerned*. David Jeremiah put this well: "If you don't worry about your children playing near traffic, you're a terrible parent. If you're not concerned about walking off the roof of a skyscraper, you'll learn the meaning of that old poster that said, 'Gravity: It's not just a good idea. It's the law.' There are things you need to be concerned about. There's a difference between carefree and careless."[5]

Why We Shouldn't Worry

As I've mentioned, in His Sermon on the Mount, Jesus said we shouldn't worry. Why? Well, *worrying is unreasonable*. In Matthew 6:25, Jesus answered two implied questions: "Who gave you your body?" and "Who determined what is necessary for you to live?" The answer is obvious: God did. He's the Creator and Provider. So, then, Jesus wanted to know, why are you worried about what you will eat or drink or wear?

If you believe God created you, then why don't you believe He will sustain you? That's the essence of what Jesus was asking. David observed in his old age that he had never "seen the righteous forsaken or his descendants begging bread" (Ps. 37:25). Why? David's son Solomon provided the answer: "The LORD will not allow the righteous to hunger" (Prov. 10:3). Our Creator God is also our Sustainer God.

Jesus also said *worrying is unfounded*. I can hear the objections now: "I know that God *can* sustain me, but *will* He sustain me?" Jesus anticipated that question and answered it in Matthew 6:26: "Look at the birds of the air, that they do not sow, nor reap nor gather in barns, and yet your heavenly Father feeds them. Are you not worth much more than they?"

In Jesus's day, you could buy two sparrows for one cent (10:29), which was one-sixteenth of the average daily wage of a laborer. Because sparrows were so cheap, sellers usually ran a deal: buy four, get one free (Luke 12:6)—not all that different from what stores do today.

Why the economic lesson in buying first-century sparrows? Because if it's true that not one sparrow can fall to the ground without the Lord's notice—even the fifth sparrow, which has zero market value—then it's equally true that the Lord will care for your needs (Matt. 10:29). God not only counts and cares for the number of sparrows in the sky, but He also counts and cares for the number of hairs on your head (v. 30). For some of us, hair counting is easier done than for others! But the point is this: if God keeps an inventory of the smallest, most incidental items, how much more is He concerned with greater items, such as whether you have enough money to pay your bills, buy groceries, or pay your rent or mortgage? God cares about birds and bouffants, beggars and billionaires.

Here's another reason not to worry: *worrying is unproductive*. It's interesting to note that Jesus used units of value and small things to ease our anxieties: coins, sparrows, and hair. Next, He used a unit of measurement: a cubit. "Who of you by being worried can add a single hour [cubit] to his life?" Jesus asked in Matthew 6:27.

A cubit was about eighteen inches, or the length of an average man's forearm. Jesus may have had two things in mind here. First, He could have been asking, "Can you stand with your back against the doorjamb, where you've marked your children's growth through the years, and worry yourself an inch taller?" The second possibility is that Jesus was asking, "Can you wake up in the morning, thinking about all the things you need to accomplish, and by worrying add an extra hour, minute, or second to your day?"

The answer to both questions is obvious. You can't worry an extra inch onto your height, and you can't worry an extra second into your day. To spend any time worrying is to be unproductive. I've discovered, in my own life and in the lives of those I've counseled, that unproductive people are usually anxious people. Productive people, on the other hand, are usually relaxed people—at peace with themselves and others.

Do you know why Jesus used things like coins and cubits, sparrows and hair to help the anxious? I think it's because things like coins and cubits are about *perspective*, and things like sparrows and hair are about *value*. When we worry, we lose perspective about what's truly valuable. God, who knows the value of all things, values sparrows. But because He also never loses perspective, He values us much more than sparrows.

Jesus isn't through instructing us on worry. He also said *worrying is unnecessary*. If God will provide food for your stomach, will He not also provide clothing for your limbs? That was Jesus's question in Matthew 6:28–30. Look at the wildflowers. They don't get up early, fight traffic, and work all hours of the day in order to buy Levis. Yet look at how beautiful they are.

Every spring, in Texas, families love to take pictures in fields of wildflowers: bluebonnets, Indian paintbrushes, Queen Anne's lace, and buttercups. These families brave bees and fire ants because the wildflowers are so beautiful. And like the lilies in the fields around Jerusalem, Texas wild-flowers are only around for a short time each year. So if you want to capture that perfect picture, you can't let the grass grow under your feet, if you know what I mean.

If God can decorate the fields with wildflowers, more abundant and beautiful than the robes and jewels in Solo-mon's closet, then worrying about what you're going to wear today or tomorrow is unnecessary. And if you're more important to God than sparrows, then it stands to reason you're more important to God than lilies. Did He make them in His own image? Did He die for their sins to save their souls? If He cares for birds by feeding them and for lilies by clothing them with beauty, but cares for you so much more, then why do you think He would neglect you? He promised, "I will never desert you, nor will I ever forsake you" (Heb. 13:5).

Finally, Jesus said *worrying is ungodly*. Let that sink in. It was natural for the unbelieving gentiles to "eagerly"—anxiously—seek and scrape for the necessities of life (Matt. 6:32). But Jesus's original audience consisted of Jews, God's special people. They should have known better. Didn't the Lord deliver them from bondage in Egypt and feed them in the desert? Not even the soles of their sandals wore out after forty years of wandering in the wilderness (Deut. 29:5). To worry is to forget God's past provision and to deny God's present power—to say that His grace is limited instead of limitless. According to Jesus, that's the mark of ungodliness.

Jesus ended this section of His sermon with a final encouraging word—one He had been trying to pound into His listeners' anxious brains throughout His message: "Your heavenly Father knows that you need all these things" (Matt. 6:32).

What We Should Do Instead of Worry

We can agree that worrying is unfounded, unproductive, unnecessary, and even ungodly. But believing these things somehow doesn't move the mountain of anxiety and bring peace to our souls. So, what can you and I do to stop worrying? Jesus provides the answer: "Seek first His kingdom and His righteousness, and all these things will be added to you. So do not worry about tomorrow; for tomorrow will care for itself. Each day has enough trouble of its own" (Matt. 6:33–34).

Instead of seeking the world's goods, seek the goods of the kingdom of God. How do you do that? Earlier in Matthew 6, Jesus taught His disciples how to pray (vv. 9–13). Buried within the Lord's Prayer is the answer to seeking

God's kingdom. First, *dedicate your life to glorifying God* (v. 9). The apostle Paul put it like this: "Whether . . . you eat or drink or whatever you do, do all to the glory of God" (1 Cor. 10:31). Second, *declare God's sovereignty over your life* (Matt. 6:10). Surrender control. Give Him free rein. Come to the point where you can say, "I am a little pencil in God's hand. He does the thinking. He does the writing."[6] Third, *determine to do God's will* (v. 10). The writer to the Hebrews concluded his letter with this benediction: "Now the God of peace . . . equip you in every good thing to do His will, working in us that which is pleasing in His sight, through Jesus Christ, to whom be the glory forever and ever. Amen" (Heb. 13:20–21).

We're to seek God's kingdom, but we're also to seek His righteousness (Matt. 6:33). In the Bible, the term *righteousness* often refers to our justification before God because of Christ's death and resurrection. That's not what Jesus had in mind in Matthew 6. He meant that we are to pursue submission to God's will so that our lives will glorify God. At the end of the day, there are only two kinds of ambition: to glorify ourselves, which leads to anxiety, or to glorify God, which leads to peace. Jesus told us to pick the latter. And if we do, then we have nothing to worry about. In the present, God will provide all we need for this life. And in the future, God will still be there, meeting all our needs.

The apostle Peter was in the audience listening to Jesus give His sermon about anxiety. It was a message he needed to hear. In his younger years, Peter was filled with worry. But when he was an older man, some thirty years after hearing Jesus's sermon, Peter showed he had learned how to deal with his anxieties. In his first letter he provided the secret to silencing our worries, and it serves as a fitting summary of Jesus's message: "Humble yourself under the mighty hand of God, that He may exalt you at the proper time, casting all your anxiety on Him, because He cares for you" (1 Pet. 5:6–7).

The Path from Anxiety to Peace

Jesus's and Peter's words ought to be enough to help us stop worrying. But some of us need additional encouragement. If that's you, I have some other practical steps you can take that will help you along the path from anxiety to peace.[7]

Repent of Known Sin

When we love anyone or anything more than God, we're committing the sin of idolatry. We are also setting the stage for a life of worry. Why? Because anything less than God can be taken from us.

I minister in one of the most prosperous areas in the country. It is also home to some of the most violent storms in the country, especially during the spring months. Dallas is at the southern end of Tornado Alley. When cool fronts sweep down from the north and collide with moist air coming off the Gulf of Mexico, large thunderstorms develop, bringing high winds, tornadoes, torrential rains, and large hail, sometimes up to the size of softballs. When one of these supercell thunderstorms develops, the people in and around Dallas get anxious. They worry about what might happen to their houses, their manicured landscapes, and their cars.

Don't misunderstand what I'm getting at here. Taking necessary precautions like bringing the car into the garage, securing lawn furniture, and having homeowners' insurance are all wise things to do. But even with those things in place, many people are consumed by worry that a storm will destroy what they've scraped together for years. There's nothing they can do about the storm, but instead of resting in the Creator's sovereignty, they become restless because creation's storm might damage or destroy their possessions.

If your anxiety is the result of trying to keep up with the Joneses, then you need to confess your sin and turn away from those attitudes and actions. After all, that's what the word *repent* means—to turn around and go in the opposite direction. When you repent, rest assured the Lord hears and forgives because "He is faithful and righteous" (1 John 1:9). Once you've repented of your sin, then follow the directions laid out in Colossians 3:1–2: "If you have been raised up with Christ, keep seeking the things above, where Christ is, seated at the right hand of God. Set your mind on the things above, not on the things that are on earth."

Remove Unnecessary Fear

Many of us feel anxious about things we know we should be doing but aren't. For example, you know you should go to the dentist, but you're afraid of what a checkup might reveal. So you keep postponing the appointment. Unfortunately, you cannot postpone your anxiety. You know that your teeth are suffering from neglect. So you continue to be infected with a low-grade case of anxiety. You don't think about your teeth every day. But on the back burner of your mind, you have just added one more source of worry.

Here are three words that will help you remove much of the anxiety in your life: *do it now!* If there is a telephone call to be made, *do it now!* If there is a difficult email to send, *do it now!* If there is an appointment to be made, *do it now!* Confront any unnecessary anxiety by dealing with it realistically. You'll find that fear is easily dissipated when confronted with truth.

Remember God's Past Faithfulness

David was no stranger to anxiety. In Psalm 3, he wrote about a particularly acute anxiety attack after his son Absalom led a national revolt against him. The first two verses reveal the depths of David's anxiety: "O LORD, how my adversaries have increased! Many are rising up against me. Many are saying of my soul, 'There is no deliverance for him in God.' Selah" (vv. 1–2).

Don't read past that little notation at the end of verse 2: "Selah." This is a musical term meaning "pause." It's an indicator to the choir director for an interlude. In this psalm, it functions as a moment for us to collect our thoughts, regain our perspective, and lay our anxieties at God's feet to find peace.

That's what David did, because in verses 3–6 he remembered God's past faithfulness, and it eased his troubled heart: "But You, O LORD, are a shield about me, my glory, and the One who lifts my head. I was crying to the LORD with my voice, and He answered me from His holy mountain. Selah. I lay down and slept; I awoke, for the LORD sustains me. I will not be afraid of ten thousands of people who have set themselves against me round about."

When David was younger, he faced Goliath without fear or worry. He said, "The LORD who delivered me from the paw of the lion and from the paw of the bear, He will deliver me from the hand of this Philistine" (1 Sam. 17:37).

To help you remember God's past faithfulness, I suggest you keep a prayer journal. Write down your requests, making sure to date them, and then record God's answer to each one. This is something I have done for years. In a notebook, I divide each page into two columns: "My Requests" and "God's Answers." Through the years, I've recorded my requests to God (and use them as a guide for my prayers). When God answers that request with a "yes" or "no," I record it under "God's Answers." Occasionally, when I'm discouraged, I flip through my journal and the cloud dissipates as I remember God's supernatural intervention in my life. And I'm equally encouraged when I read some of the "no" answers to my prayers and see how God had a better plan for my life than I could've ever imagined.

Remain in Contact with God

The three greatest antidotes to anxiety are found in Philippians 4:6–9. First, if we want to get rid of anxiety, we must *pray persistently*. Paul said in verses 6–7, "Be anxious for nothing, but in everything by prayer and supplication with thanksgiving let your requests be made known to God. And the peace of God, which surpasses all comprehension, will guard your hearts and your minds in Christ Jesus."

Second, to drive anxiety from our lives, we must *think truthfully*—that's Paul's point in verse 8: "Finally, brethren, whatever is true, whatever is honorable, whatever is right, whatever is pure, whatever is lovely, whatever is of good repute, if there is any excellence and if anything worthy of praise, dwell on these things." If you want to experience the peace of God, think on the things of God. The best way to do that is to spend time in the Word of God. And when you do, you just might run across this promise: "Those who love Your law have great peace, and nothing causes them to stumble" (Ps. 119:165).

Third, to remove the poison of anxiety, we must *conduct ourselves consistently*—that's what Paul is getting at in Philippians 4:9: "The things you have learned and received and heard and seen in me, practice these things, and the God of peace will be with you." When our conduct isn't consistent with what we know to be true, the result is fear. Proverbs 28:1 says, "The wicked flee when no one is pursuing." Are you running scared from something? Are you afraid that you might be found out? Is there anything you need to stop doing—or start doing?

There's probably at least one thing you need to start doing. We all need to be better at imitating Christ. We need to get serious about glorifying God, turning control over to Him, and doing His will—no matter what that is. If we spent a little more time practicing what we know to be true, we would discover our anxiety levels decreasing and our peace levels increasing. That's the only way to live!

God may or may not deliver you out of your circumstances, but He promises to give you a supernatural peace of mind in the midst of those circumstances. "There may be greater sins than worry," theologian William Barclay wrote, "but very certainly there is no more disabling sin."[8] That's why we must turn to God whenever we encounter the mountain of anxiety. He's the only one who can give us the peace we long for.

FOUR

MOVING FROM
DISCOURAGEMENT
TO HOPE

―――――――――

THOMAS EDISON WAS THE INVENTOR of the incandescent light bulb, the telegraph, the phonograph, the microphone, and the moving picture camera, as well as many other devices that transformed the world. He lived in New Jersey and was dubbed the "Wizard of Menlo Park."

What makes Edison memorable to me is not so much his array of inventions as his attitude when things didn't work out. For example, while attempting to create a storage battery, he tried ten thousand different experiments. All failures. But he didn't see it that way. He reportedly said, "I have not failed. I have just found 10,000 ways that won't work."[1]

But even that determination and optimism pale in comparison to what happened one night in December 1914. Ten years of trial and error on the development of his storage battery left Edison and his company on the edge of financial ruin. And if it hadn't been for the profits from his moving picture and recording inventions, Edison would have been forced to close his doors and lay off his staff. Things could hardly look worse—until the worst happened.

On that December night, the film room spontaneously burst into flames. According to Edison's son Charles, "Within moments all the packing compounds, celluloid for records, film, and other flammable goods had gone up with a whoosh."[2] The fire spread quickly through the building. Fire departments from eight neighboring towns converged on Edison's laboratory, but the intensity of the fire was so great and the water pressure was so low the firefighters might as well have been using squirt guns. There wasn't anything anyone could do but watch the building and its contents go up in flames.

Then it dawned on Charles: he hadn't seen his father. Charles wondered, "Would his will be broken?" Edison was sixty-seven at the time, "no age to begin anew." Then Charles saw his father running across the yard. "'Where's Mom?' Edison shouted, 'Go get her! Tell her to get her friends! They'll never see a fire like this again!'"

The next day, Edison called his employees together and announced they were rebuilding. He delegated responsibilities to lease machine shops and obtain a wrecking crane from the Erie Railroad. "Then, almost as an afterthought he added, 'Oh, by the way. Anybody know where we can get some money?'" Edison concluded, "You can always make capital out of disaster. . . . We've just cleared out a bunch of old rubbish. We'll build bigger and better on the ruins." Then Charles said, "With that he rolled up his coat, curled up on a table, and immediately fell asleep."[3]

I wonder, how would you respond if you drove into your neighborhood and saw fire trucks and smoke rising over the housetops, then realized the house they were dousing was yours? Would your reaction be like that of Edison, who watched his business go up in flames? Or would your reaction be something closer to that of Job's wife, who told her husband to "curse God and die" after he had lost his children, his livelihood, and his health (Job 2:9)?

I've always thought preachers like me have been too hard on Mrs. Job. After all, she also lost her children and security, and for all she knew, she might lose her husband too. It was natural for her to be distraught. We all think we'd be like Job and declare, as he did, "Shall we indeed accept good from God and not accept adversity? . . . The LORD gave and the LORD has taken away. Blessed be the name of the LORD" (2:10; 1:21). But let's get real. Chances are, you and I wouldn't respond like that. Most of us would be more like Mrs. Job. You don't believe me? Think about what your initial reaction would be to one or more of these life-altering events:

- A job loss
- A missed promotion
- A miscarriage
- A divorce
- Discovering your spouse is having an affair
- The death of a loved one

Would you respond with sunny optimism or with pessimism? We're easily discouraged—and not just by the big

85

things in life. When's the last time you tried to learn something new and gave up in frustration? Or tried to help your child with their "new" math? Have you ever tried to learn the guitar and put it down because you had difficulty getting your fingers in all those weird shapes or because your fingertips burned like a thousand fire ants were gnawing on them? Have you given up on your French cooking class because you keep burning the soufflé?

Discouragement is like a disease eating away at the hope in your heart. If it persists, it becomes resistant to the encouragement we often get from others. It's the rare person indeed who can pull themselves out of the doldrums by their own bootstraps. Thankfully, the Lord isn't on the sidelines merely cheering on those who face the mountain of discouragement. As we'll see, there is no "You can do it. I believe in you. Get up and brush the dust off and get going" rah-rahing from Him. No. What you get from Jesus is someone who is conquering the mountain with you and helping you become invincible.

Discouragement: A Definition

Webster defines *discourage* as "to deprive of courage or confidence"—to be "disheartened."[4] The New Testament uses three Greek words that all get at the same basic meaning of becoming disheartened, dispirited, and discouraged.[5] But I think we could add a few other *D* words that describe being discouraged: *demoralized*, *dismayed*, *distraught*, *depressed*, *defeated*, and *despairing*. These are all things we feel when the realities of life hijack us.

At the beginning of 2020, almost everyone in the world experienced collective discouragement and despair. A new virus called COVID-19 (coronavirus) swept across borders and nations, infecting millions and killing hundreds of thousands. In an effort to stem the spread of the disease, people sheltered in their homes, separated from extended families, friends, neighbors, and coworkers for months on end. Businesses shut down; schools sent children and college students home; churches closed their doors and held services online. Aside from the economic devastation caused by the pandemic and the lives lost, mental health problems skyrocketed. Police departments all over the United States reported increased domestic violence calls. There were fears that alcohol and drug addictions would be on the rise, as would suicide rates. People panicked, buying up toilet paper, hand sanitizer, meat, and milk. And face masks became a part of our wardrobe. As the pandemic wore on, month after month, people became discouraged and demoralized, wondering whether life would ever get back to normal.

Causes of Discouragement

Discouragement can be debilitating, but it doesn't just develop out of nowhere. Discouragement is always a result of some cause, and I've identified seven of them.

Unresolved Anger

It has been said that depression is anger turned inward. Usually, we deal with our anger by venting—blowing up at whoever or whatever is responsible for turning our day on its head. Sometimes others are at fault, but sometimes we are at fault. When it's others, we may not feel the freedom to express how we feel. We may fear that a loved one will leave us or that an employer might fire us. So we bottle up our anger. When our problems are a result of our own sinfulness or foolishness, we kick ourselves internally. If we don't deal with our anger, whether directed at another person, a situation, or ourselves, discouragement can flood into our lives like water from a broken pipe.

Unrealistic Anxiety

As we saw in the previous chapter, nothing can sap our strength and make us discouraged like worry. That was part of the Old Testament prophet Elijah's problem after his spiritual victory on Mount Carmel. He had an emotional breakdown when Jezebel threatened his life (1 Kings 19:1–3). He was physically exhausted, but he was also worried about what Jezebel would do to him. What made his anxiety unrealistic was the fact that God had already protected him from the evil schemes of her priests, who had carried swords with them to Mount Carmel. Why did Elijah now think God wouldn't protect him from the queen's bounty hunters?

Unrealized Aims

British essayist Thomas Carlyle wrote, "A man without a purpose is like a ship without a rudder."[6] In other words, a man or woman without a clear purpose in life is cast adrift. Is there anything more discouraging than going through life aimlessly? Solomon declared that life is meaningless because it's short and hard to understand (Eccles. 1:2). For some, life is certainly short, but that doesn't mean it has to be hard to understand. Carlyle continued, "Have a purpose in life . . . and having it, throw such strength of mind and muscle into your work as God has given you."[7] That's good advice to follow if you want to avoid discouragement.

Unrepented Guilt

We explored the difference between true guilt and false guilt in chapter 2. False guilt, or misplaced guilt, is a tool Satan uses to convince us that our past sins, though they have been confessed and forgiven by God, are really not forgiven—that God still holds us accountable for the sins of yesterday. This is a cunning deception because God does hold us responsible for our unrepented *sins*—true guilt—which rightfully leads to discouragement. That's what David was feeling when he wrote, "When I kept silent about my sin, my body wasted away through my groaning all day long" (Ps. 32:3). But Satan attempts to use false guilt—sins we've already confessed—to throw our emotions into a tailspin. In the first instance, we should repent of our sins, as David did (v. 5). In the second instance, we should remember that God has cast our sins "into the depths of the sea" (Mic. 7:19) and refuse to allow Satan to go fishing for them.

Unrelenting Grief

Being separated from a loved one by death, defection, or distance is a prime source of discouragement. It's normal for us to feel distraught when we're separated from those we love. When Jesus saw the tomb of His dead friend Lazarus, He wept (John 11:35). But then He dried His eyes and got on with life by bringing Lazarus back to life. Activity is a great antidote for discouragement and depression. And so is remembering this promise: "Weeping may last for the night, but a shout of joy comes in the morning" (Ps. 30:5).

Unrestrained Infirmities

Aging is often accompanied by discouragement. When you consider the number of losses an elderly person endures during a long life, it's easy to understand why he or she might become disheartened. But family and friends aren't the only losses we experience as we age. Health declines, eyesight weakens, hearing fades, hands shake, and knees wobble.

Unrectified Imbalances

Doctors tell us that sometimes a chemical imbalance in the brain can be a source of despondence. For example, an imbalance of sodium chloride in the brain cells hinders the transfer of messages from one cell to another. Although this isn't the most common cause for being discouraged, it's a possibility that should be checked out by a physician if you or someone you love continues to struggle with discouragement and depression.

A Drama Starring Discouragement

In the history of ancient Israel, two events more than any others shaped the people's character. Both had happy endings but began in trauma. The first was the four hundred years of Egyptian slavery, followed by the exodus and the possessing of the promised land. The second was the seventy years of exile in Babylon, followed by the return to Jerusalem and the rebuilding of the temple.

When the Israelites returned to Jerusalem, they were surrounded by enemies who constantly nipped at their heels. No matter which direction they turned, the Israelites had to fend off attackers. Nehemiah said these people "conspired together to come and fight against Jerusalem and to cause a disturbance in it" (Neh. 4:8). The attacks weren't physical; they were verbal and were meant to discourage the people from rebuilding the city walls. The attacks had their intended effect. It's difficult not to become discouraged when you hear disheartening messages day in and day out. This is why, if you're prone to discouragement, you should pick your friends carefully. You want to have positive people in your life, those who will encourage you with words of "grace, as though seasoned with salt" (Col. 4:6). Negative people will discourage you with graceless words that leave only bitterness.

The Israelites didn't get to choose their neighbors, so they couldn't escape their hurtful words. And over time, the whispering campaign against the construction projects proved successful. Nehemiah told us what happened when these conspirators infiltrated the workers and spread the poison of discouragement. In the fourth chapter of his book of the Bible, we find the construction at the halfway point, and the reasons the Israelites were discouraged are just as applicable for our own discouragement today.

The People Were Drained

Green Bay Packers coach Vince Lombardi famously noted, "Fatigue makes cowards of us all."[8] Nehemiah observed the same thing. He wrote, "The strength of the burden bearers is failing" (Neh. 4:10). The Hebrew word for "failing" (*kasal*) means "to stumble, stagger, or totter." After fifty-two days of backbreaking labor, the wall was only halfway complete. And though they "had a mind to work," the Israelites were physically and emotionally drained (v. 6). The excitement of rebuilding Jerusalem was beginning to waver. If you've ever led a big project, you know something about this. After a while, enthusiasm gives way to disillusionment, cheer gives way to complaints, and encouragement gives way to discouragement.

The midpoint in any major project is a dangerous place to be. The energy at the beginning lags in the middle when what's before us, that which is yet to be accomplished, looks greater than what's behind us, that which we've already accomplished. This is the moment when discouragement comes around and says, "Hang it up! You'll never finish. You just don't have it in you."

I am well acquainted with the mountain of discouragement. It paid my church and me a visit a number of years ago when we demolished some old buildings on our downtown campus and built our new worship center. The excitement on the day we imploded those old buildings and the day the construction crew began erecting new beams outlining the footprint of our new building soon gave way as the months dragged on and we couldn't tell much difference between what was finished yesterday and what was unfinished today. It's at moments like these when we need to find a new source of hope and courage to keep our shoulder to the wheel, pushing forward.

The People Were Disgruntled

When you live with teenagers, the middle section of Nehemiah 4:10 can become your life verse: "Yet there is much rubbish." At least that's what I've been told. Since our girls were pretty fastidious, even in their teens—a trait they came by honestly from their mother and father—Amy and I never had to hang up that verse in our home. But I know others who have. I've had friends describe their children as Hansel and Gretel: you could follow the breadcrumbs to where they were by tracking their clothes and backpacks from the front door to their bedrooms.

My friends never used the word *disgruntled* when describing their reaction whenever they opened the door to their child's bedroom and a mound came spilling out, but that's exactly what the Israelites felt as they looked around the city of Jerusalem. Sure, a good portion of the wall was finished, but there was a lot of rubble lying around—broken bricks, buckets of mortar, and debris of every kind.

Did you catch the little word *yet* at the beginning of verse 10? It's significant. It connects the idea of there being much rubbish to the previous sentence describing how the wall builders were becoming drained. Much work had been accomplished—half a wall around an entire city is no small feat—*yet* there was still so much rubble on the construction site.

Rubbish and construction are perfect complements to each other. When we imploded those old buildings on our church campus, mountains of rubble were left behind. I thought, *Boy, it will take months and a fleet of trucks to clear this junk away*. It did take a fleet of trucks, but it didn't take months. In no time the ground was clean and ready to begin construction on our new worship center. But then the builders created new piles of rubble. You didn't dare walk anywhere close to the construction site without a hard hat and steel-toed boots. There was no telling whether a sawed-off board might fall on your head or you might step on a rusty nail. Everyone at the church was excited when the construction began, but after a while, things seemed to bog down. Permits were delayed, wrong materials were delivered, and weather halted work. As things dragged on, I began to grow discouraged, wondering, *Will the building ever be completed? Will we ever get this place cleaned up?* Of course, slowly—and surely—the building was finished. And when it was, I was no longer discouraged.

The People Were Dejected

We know from Nehemiah 4:10 that the people were *drained* from their hard labor ("The strength of the burden bearers is failing") and that they were *disgruntled* ("Yet there is much rubbish"). The final sentence in that verse tells us they were also *dejected*: "And we ourselves are unable to rebuild the wall."

Being physically and emotionally drained, coupled with an attitude of being disgruntled, is a perfect recipe for dejection. Weary people are whiny people. Though the Israelites had "a heart for the work" (v. 6 MSG), they began to complain: "We're in over our heads, we can't build this wall" (v. 10 MSG). In other words, they were saying, "It's too hard."

Every now and then, everyone has an unfinished wall in their lives—a house that needs cleaning, a relationship that needs repair, or an education that needs completing. Difficulties are just part of living in a fallen world. The key to keeping yourself from losing your grip on hope and sliding into discouragement is handling those difficulties with a positive attitude and a proper perspective. If you let negative thoughts dominate your thinking, then your perspective becomes distorted: "Look at all the rubble in my life." A distorted perspective, if not refocused, leads to a dejected spirit: "Life stinks!" And a dejected spirit leads to discouragement: "I can't do this."

The People Were Distressed

If you add up the first three reasons for discouragement, you get a depressing outcome: *distress.* That's exactly where the Jews who were building the wall in Jerusalem ended up. Nehemiah recorded in his journal what their detractors were saying—and what the people believed: "Our enemies said, 'They will not know or see until we come among them, kill them and put a stop to the work.' [Then] the Jews who lived near them came and told us ten times, 'They will come up against us from every place where you may turn'" (Neh. 4:11–12).

All the Israelites could see was a distressful future. I'm convinced that nothing discourages us and derails our work for God more than negative comments. Threats, warnings, gossip, and whisper campaigns are all spirit killers. Criticism can contaminate the most courageous heart.

Are you dealing with a critic in your life right now? If so, you know what I'm talking about. Perhaps the *drip, drip, drip* of criticism is eroding your heart, and you feel yourself slipping into distress. Such denigration can come from a coworker or a boss. But the most dangerous criticism comes from loved ones.

Criticism is only one form of negative talk. Another form comes from people who prey on your fears, especially about the future. Every parent who has a student in college worries that his or her child will graduate and move back into the house. What these parents really fear for is their child's future security.

Security is a human desire that cannot be ignored or minimized. But neither should we confuse our true source of security with a well-paying job. Writing against the sin of presumption and for surrendering our life's decisions to the Lord, James said, "To one who knows the right thing to do and does not do it, to him it is sin" (James 4:17). You and I are to do what God has called us to do, and not let the criticism of others or the uncertainty of the future cause us distress and rob us of our hearts.

The Path from Discouragement to Hope

Rebuilding the wall around Jerusalem proved more challenging than the Israelites thought, not only because there was so much work to be accomplished but also because their enemies did all they could to halt construction. Fortunately, the Lord appointed a foreman who knew as much about encouraging others as he did about building walls.

You cannot ignore discouragement and assume it will somehow magically disappear. Flat tires remain flat no matter how much you pray. Likewise, pray as you might, discouraged people remain discouraged. Flat tires need to be reinflated, and discouraged people need to be encouraged. Nehemiah knew that and took five decisive actions to restore the heart of the people—steps you and I can (and should) take today whenever we, too, encounter the mountain of discouragement and want to start on the path to hope.

Find Encouragement in Your Family

I know that not everyone has a healthy family of origin. Some of us had absent fathers, even if our dads came home after work every day. Others had parents or family members who struggled with addiction or had to endure abusive behavior. But did you marry into a good family? Or do you have close friends who support you? If so, then they're as good as family.

If you're wrestling with discouragement, the first place to turn is to your family or to friends who are like family to you. Notice what Nehemiah did when the people grew disheartened about the construction and about those spreading threats: "I stationed men in the lowest parts of the space behind the wall, the exposed places, and I stationed the people *in families* with their swords, spears and bows" (Neh. 4:13). When the excitement of the project was in full swing, workers fanned out all over the city and put their shoulders to the work. But when excitement gave way to exasperation, Nehemiah's first act was to redistribute the workforce into family units.

Why is this significant? Next to God, our primary source of security is our family. Look at verse 13 again. Nehemiah brought families back together to work on the wall "with their swords, spears and bows." When my girls were younger and living at home, one of my main responsibilities was to protect them—to wield my sword, throw my spear, or shoot my bow at anyone or anything that sought to harm Julia or Dorothy. And now, even though they've grown and moved out of the house, I still see myself as their protector. Whether it's a hostile boss, a dishonest repair person, or a flat tire, my first instinct is to jump in and shield my daughters from anything that would harm them.

Remember God Is on Your Side

Turning to your family first isn't to say that your family is more important than God when it comes to conquering the mountain of discouragement. Nehemiah was a realist. Though the Lord had done an amazing work in bringing the people back into the land after seventy years of exile, it's hard to forget a seventy-year history of God's discipline, especially if you're already feeling defeated. Sometimes we need people to point us to the One who is the true source of encouragement. When we do, we can look to how Nehemiah described our God: "Do not be afraid of them; remember the Lord who is great and awesome, and fight for your brothers, your sons, your daughters, your wives and your houses" (Neh. 4:14).

The words *great* and *awesome* communicate the idea that in light of the magnitude of God, everyone and everything else is puny by comparison. Because of His enormous bigness, we have nothing to fear from things or people that amount to little more than a fuzz ball on the pages of history, easily flicked away by His finger or blown off by His breath—*puff!*

Reading God's Word is one of the best ways to remember how great and awesome He is. Nothing will inflate sagging spirits with hope more than encountering Him in Scripture. I know there are times when reading your Bible is the last thing you want to do, especially when you're discouraged. But that's just when you should crack open your Bible! When your heart is broken and your spirit is low is the perfect time for an infusion of hope and healing. And when you find a passage that raises your spirits, commit it to memory. The next time you find your courage flagging, the Lord will help you recall it.

Another way to remember that God is on your side is by meditating on who He is. This is what Nehemiah was helping the people do by referring to God as "great and awesome." Next time you hear a favorite hymn or worship song, pay careful attention to the lyrics that extol something wonderful about God, and concentrate on that attribute. Maybe you're an outdoor person. Get outside and spend an hour watching the stars and thinking about the One who holds each star in the palm of His hand. Before you know it, you'll find discouragement replaced by hope.

Do the Work God Has Given You

If we want to move the mountain of discouragement, we have to do the work God has given us. That's the balancing act Nehemiah encouraged the people to strike in verses 15–18 of chapter 4.

God was certainly on the side of the Israelites who were working on the wall. Nehemiah said, "God had frustrated [the] plan" of their enemies (v. 15). But that didn't mean the dangers confronting them in Jerusalem were figments of their imagination. The threats against their lives were real, so Nehemiah divided his workforce into construction crews and security guards. "From that day on," Nehemiah wrote, "half of my servants carried on the work while half of them held the spears, the shields, the bows and the breastplates" (v. 16). And that's not all. Even the builders were armed for battle: "Those who were rebuilding the wall and those who carried burdens took their load with one hand doing the work and the other holding a weapon. As for the builders, each wore his sword girded at his side as he built, while the trumpeter stood near me" (vv. 17–18).

If that's not a picture of the Christian life, I don't know what is. We are to "walk by faith, not by sight" (2 Cor. 5:7).

But we're also to be about the work God has given to us. We cannot let discouragement cause us to put down the trowel and drop the bricks. There's work to be done—fueled by faith but accomplished by action. And it's time to get at it.

Enlist Others to Help You

Nehemiah brought families together to work as units, which offered security and encouragement as each family took ownership of their section of the wall as well as the protection of their family members. But that didn't mean these families weren't vulnerable to attack. They were scattered over a construction site that covered two and a half miles. So Nehemiah created an ancient early warning system. But instead of that annoying blaring sound that comes through our televisions and radios when a tornado or other severe weather is approaching, Nehemiah appointed a bugler to alert the people to danger. Here's how he put it: "I said to the nobles, the officials and the rest of the people, 'The work is great and extensive, and we are separated on the wall far from one another. At whatever place you hear the sound of the trumpet, rally to us there. Our God will fight for us'" (Neh. 4:19–20).

In the face of danger, Nehemiah's order established the *place* where the people could rally together. And his command also established a *principle*: never fight your battles alone. This is why Solomon said, "A person standing alone can be attacked and defeated, but two can stand back-to-back and conquer. Three are even better, for a triple-braided cord is not easily broken" (Eccles. 4:12 NLT). Solomon also wrote, "A friend loves at all times, and a brother is born for adversity" (Prov. 17:17). When you're facing adversity and your heart begins to sink under a tidal wave of despair, call for help, because the old cliché is true: a friend in need is a friend indeed.

Serve Another Person in Need

Discouraged people need friends to come to their rescue. That's true of you as well as others. And when others are struggling with discouragement, one of the best things you can do, even if you're facing your own discouraging days, is to be their friend.

Notice what Nehemiah said next: "So we carried on the work with half of them holding spears from dawn until the stars appeared. At that time I also said to the people, 'Let each man with his servant spend the night within Jerusalem so that they may be a guard for us by night and a laborer by day'" (Neh. 4:21–22).

Nehemiah called on the people to take around-the-clock shifts to protect those in need of sleep. These night guards patrolled the wall in pairs, making sure vandals didn't tear down what had been built that day. And then, during the day, they picked up their trowels while others stood guard. Night and day, the workers rotated in and out, some laying brick and some standing guard. And Nehemiah rolled up his sleeves to demonstrate what we call servant leadership. He wrote, "So neither I, my brothers, my servants, nor the men of the guard who followed me removed our clothes, each took his weapon even to the water" (v. 23).

Every leader should follow Nehemiah's example. And so should every Christian, whether you call yourself a leader or not. The ancient Israelites served one another in both guard duty and construction work. This reminds me of a service station sign I came across in one of my travels: "We will crawl under your car oftener and get ourselves dirtier than any of our competition." That's not a bad definition for Christian service.

When is the last time you served someone? Or are you one of those folks who thinks everyone should serve you? If you're facing discouraging days, one of the greatest things you can do to lift your spirits is to serve another person in need. A friend of mine once said, "When you give yourself away, you get more in return than you ever give away." Find someone you can serve this week.

A Word of Encouragement for the Discouraged

One of the greatest examples of an encourager I have witnessed is my daughter Dorothy, who demonstrated many of the steps Nehemiah laid out for us to move the mountain of discouragement. She was having lunch with her older sister, Julia. As I mentioned earlier, Julia and her husband, Ryan, had difficulty getting pregnant, and keeping the pregnancies was more difficult. Through infertility and then multiple miscarriages, Julia and Ryan had become discouraged, coming to believe they would never have a family of their own. Then one day at lunch, Dorothy said something her sister would never forget. Julia described this moment in her book, *Pray Big Things*:

> She looked at me and said, "Julia, I think something really big is about to happen." This was a year before the triplets were born, before my dad became a presidential adviser, and before Ryan and I were cast in a reality TV show that gave us

the ability to talk about Jesus Christ on a national platform. How did Dorothy know?

Dorothy is not some kind of modern-day prophetess, but she understands the spiritual progression of events. Temptation, struggles, trials, and persecution usually come before blessing. If we figure out that sequence, we will not be swayed in our beliefs. While the trials will be hard, our victory is certain.[9]

Whether from a sister, a friend, or even a total stranger, a simple word of encouragement can lighten the heaviest heart. If the mountain of discouragement threatens to overshadow you, find someone you can serve and encourage as, together, you walk the path to hope.

FIVE

MOVING FROM FEAR
TO COURAGE

A COLLEAGUE OF MINE grew up around bugs. His father was a biology teacher and kept a collection of butterflies, moths, beetles, spiders, and even cockroaches pinned to a corkboard. In the family I grew up in, we didn't collect bugs; we killed them.

Of course, when you become a parent and a cockroach scurries across the floor, after the initial terror, 911 is alerted. In Texas, we have cockroaches you could throw a saddle on and ride around the kitchen. So whenever the call went out for me to rescue my wife and daughters, I geared up for war. Stepping onto the battlefield with a can of Raid in one hand and a shoe in the other, I always tried to remember this piece of advice—and so should you, if you're the one who has to perform bug patrol in your home: it's best to keep a stiff upper lip when doing battle with a six-legged critter that walks around (and sometimes flies) in armor.

Squaring off with my enemy, I would turn to my wife and say with an air of bravado, "He's more scared of you than you are him." Then I'd glance back at the roach with a snarl. He'd try to scurry away, but I'd unleash chemical warfare. My enemy would stagger and stumble . . . and then flip on his back, six spindly legs pointing to the sky.

At this point, you'd think I'd get a medal for heroism. But my job wasn't done yet. I couldn't leave the body of my vanquished foe lying on the battlefield. I'd grab a broom and dustbin, praying that he didn't pull a Lazarus on me before I dumped him into the trash. If he did, it would expose to the watching eyes of my loved ones the truth about who I really was: a coward who can run out of the kitchen faster than a gazelle!

Fear is a natural part of life, but it wasn't part of God's original design. In the garden of Eden, Adam had no fear of lions and tigers and bears—or of cockroaches, if there were any before the fall. Though fear can be useful, providing a surge of adrenaline that makes us acutely aware of dangerous situations so we can take appropriate actions, chronic fear can paralyze us from moving forward into the blessed life God intends for us.

Some Facts about Fear

A flood of adrenaline has helped save countless people thrust into fearful circumstances. When threatening situations cross our path, our physical response is fight or flight. We will either stand our ground and reason our way through whatever circumstance is confronting us, or we'll panic and run. But as I explained in my book *Courageous*, there is a third response: freeze. We can be so mentally and emotionally overwhelmed that we become the proverbial deer in the headlights.[1] When this happens, the stress level induced by fear is off the charts. And if it continues in a prolonged state, then there can be severe physical, emotional, and spiritual consequences.[2]

Physical Consequences of Fear

Fear has an icy grip. When left unattended, it will grab you by the throat and threaten to choke the life out of you. According to medical experts, the physical effects of fear include a suppressed immune system, a disturbance in the sleep/wake cycle, eating disorders, headaches and migraines, muscle aches and fibromyalgia, body aches and chronic pain, difficulty breathing and asthma, and learning difficulties.

Emotional Consequences of Fear

Scholar Edith Hamilton wrote, "Fear is of all emotions the most brutalizing."[3] It's the feeling of being held under and suffocating, creating greater fear—of terror and panic—and will damage you emotionally if you fail to get a grip on it. Fear induces mood swings, obsessive-compulsive thoughts, chronic anxiety, the prevalent thought that you're a victim, and an inability to develop feelings of love and compassion.

Spiritual Consequences of Fear

We are more than our bodies and our feelings; we're also spiritual beings. Chronic fear affects us spiritually just as much as it affects us physically and emotionally. Its effects can include bitterness toward God and others; loss of trust in God's goodness, mercy, and grace; and confusion as to what God is doing in our lives.

Soviet dissident and Nobel Prize–winning novelist Aleksandr Solzhenitsyn, who spent years in one of Stalin's gulags, asked a penetrating question about fear: "If we live in a state of constant fear, can we remain human?"[4] The implied answer is no, because we no longer live as we're intended—as the image bearers of God who were made to enjoy the blessed life with our heads up and shoulders back. Rather, we live like beasts that run and hide at every sound and shadow. This is not the way it was meant to be; this is not the way it has to be.

An Ancient Game of *Fear Factor*

When God delivered His people out of Egyptian bondage, He did so with awe-inspiring miracles. The ten plagues were just a warm-up act. He parted the Red Sea and held back Pharaoh's chariots so His people could cross on dry ground. He then drowned Pharaoh's army in the same sea when He let loose the dam holding the waters back. He led the Israelites through the desert with a pillar of cloud by day and a pillar of fire by night. He fed them with manna and made water gush from a rock. He gave them the Ten Commandments, written by His own finger, and promised them a home and a future in a land "flowing with milk and honey" (Exod. 3:17).

The people grumbled incessantly, and God had to discipline them. Yet the miracles kept coming. In fact, the miracles were so frequent the people got used to them. You may know the saying "Familiarity breeds contempt." But before contempt there's complacency—the ho-hum attitude that's satisfied with the status quo. If we're not careful, then complacency will breed cynicism.

This is what happened to the Israelites when they reached the threshold of the promised land. Camped just outside in the oasis of Kadesh Barnea, they no longer viewed God as the awe-inspiring miracle worker. He had become small in their eyes compared to the giants of the land, who struck terror in their hearts.

The Requirements of God

Before the people went weak-kneed, God commanded Moses to select twelve men to spy out the land. He said, "Send out for yourself men so that they may spy out the land of Canaan, which I am going to give to the sons of Israel; you shall send a man from each of their fathers' tribes, every one a leader among them" (Num. 13:2).

God commissioned these spies for two reasons. First, *they were to report the benefits of the land so the people would be encouraged to move forward.* Moses told the spies to pay careful attention to the quality of the land and, if at all possible, to bring back some of the fruit (vv. 17–20).

Leaders who want to move their people into the future need to constantly be painting a picture of what the future could look like to motivate them to make the needed sacrifices and changes to move forward. When I was pastor of First Baptist Church in Wichita Falls, Texas, we worshiped in a sanctuary that was nearly a century old. I knew we needed to build a new worship center, but the challenge was to help the congregation understand it needed to be done.

I realized the only way to do that was visually. The problem was that the church didn't have large IMAG screens at the time. In fact, few churches did in those days. So, the first thing I did was to take up a special offering to purchase an IMAG system. I told the congregation the new technology would enhance the worship experience, and it did. But it also provided a visual tool to show the congregation what a new sanctuary could look like.

Moses didn't have an IMAG system to help the children of Israel visualize what the promised land looked like. But he did have spies who could bring back a verbal report and a sample of fruit to encourage the people to move forward with confidence.

Second, *they were to identify the obstacles in possessing the land so the people could develop a strategy.* Moses asked the spies to find out what the people looked like—were they strong or weak, few or many? And what about their cities—were they built like "open camps or with fortifications" (vv. 18–19)?

God had promised the land to the Israelites, but they were going to have to fight for every square inch of it. Obviously, God could have removed all the obstacles so they could possess it without lifting a finger, but He understood the importance of making sure they had skin in the game. For example, a father might have the financial resources to give his child a car, but he still might say, "I will put up half the money if you earn the other half." Why? Because a wise father knows if his child has a stake in the purchase, he or she will appreciate the car more and take better care of it.

This is a theme we find throughout Scripture—almost every worthwhile achievement in life is a joint effort between

God and us. That includes building a successful marriage, family, and career. It's not that God *couldn't* do it by Himself, but He wants us to be a part of whatever project He's involved in. The only accomplishment God absolutely refuses to allow us to play a part in is our salvation. That is totally a gift from God and includes no contribution from us, so that we can never take credit for it, as Paul said in Ephesians 2:8–9: "For by grace you have been saved through faith; and that not of yourselves, it is the gift of God; not as a result of works, so that no one may boast."

Some people believe it's unspiritual for Christians or a church to spend time strategizing for the future. "You should be praying instead of planning," they say. But that doesn't square with the Bible. Solomon said, "The plans of the diligent lead surely to advantage, but everyone who is hasty comes surely to poverty" (Prov. 21:5). God's plan was for the Israelites to spy out the land so Moses could plan the conquest.

The Report of the Spies

This mission to spy out the land lasted forty days (Num. 13:25). The spies came back with pomegranates, figs, and a cluster of grapes so large two men carried it on a pole between them (v. 23). The people were amazed at the sight of the fruit, and the spies reported that the land "certainly does flow with milk and honey" (v. 27).

If they had stopped right there, all would have been well. But they didn't. You've probably run across those people who just don't know when to shut their mouths. They keep talking and talking, and they make matters worse. That's what happened here. As excited as the spies were to talk about the abundance of the land, they were just as excited to talk about the giants who lived there. "Nevertheless, the people . . . are strong, and the cities are fortified and very large" (v. 28). And if that wasn't enough, the spies went on: "Moreover, we saw the descendants of Anak there," as well as the "Nephilim" (vv. 28, 33).

Anak means "strong-necked." Moses, the author of Numbers, tells us that the sons of Anak were a "part of the Nephilim" (v. 33). The only other occurrence of *Nephilim* is in Genesis 6:4, where the word describes the offspring of giants. Whoever the Nephilim were in Genesis, they were destroyed by the flood. The reference to the Nephilim in Numbers is merely a description of their size—they were giant-like.

The sight of these giants terrified ten of the spies. "We became like grasshoppers in our own sight," they reported, "and so we were in their sight" (v. 33). Interesting insight here: how other people perceive us is often dictated by how we perceive ourselves. If you view yourself as inferior, then other people will look at you as inferior. The term *self-esteem* has been discounted among some Christians as self-help mumbo-jumbo, but it doesn't have to be. It's important to view ourselves as God views us—as people of worth because He created us, loves us, and sent His Son to redeem us.

What makes the story of the spies interesting is that their assessment of the situation wasn't at all unanimous. Two of the twelve men, who saw the same people and the same land, came back with a strikingly different report.

The Reaction of the Israelites

Though the promised land was filled with Hittites and Jebusites and Amorites and Canaanites (Num. 13:29), Caleb was gung-ho for marching in. Look at what he said: "We should by all means go up and take possession of it, for we will surely overcome it" (v. 30). Caleb was full of courage and faith.

Too bad his other companions, except Joshua, were full of cowardice and faithlessness. "We are not able to go up against the people," they protested, "for they are too strong for us . . . and the land through which we have gone . . . is a land that devours its inhabitants" (vv. 31–32). And just in case the people didn't get the message, the ten spies put a finer point on it: "all the people whom we saw in it are men of great size" (v. 32).

So, what did the people do? They decided to fire Moses and appoint another leader who would take them back to Egypt. But of course it wasn't just Moses who got them into this pickle; it was God's fault as well. They would've been better off dying as slaves in Egypt or rotting in the desert than having to face giants in the promised land (14:1–4).

I'm sure Moses was worn out leading these complaining, faithless, and fearful people. I mean, who wouldn't be? But Joshua and Caleb had really had enough. They tried one last time to reason with their frightened brothers and sisters: "The land which we passed through to spy out is an exceedingly good land. If the Lord is pleased with us, then He will bring us into this land and give it to us—a land which flows with milk and honey. Only do not rebel against the Lord; and do not fear the people of the land, for they will be our prey. Their protection has been removed from them, and the Lord is with us; do not fear them" (vv. 7–9).

It was a nice speech, but it fell on deaf ears. The people weren't afraid of Joshua and Caleb, and they picked up stones to kill them (v. 10). Could you imagine what would've happened if the people of England had responded to Winston Churchill like they did to Caleb and Joshua after Churchill tried to rouse them with his speech: "Victory—victory at all costs, victory in spite of all terror, victory, however long and hard the road may be; for without victory, there is no survival"?[5] England would have fallen to Hitler and the Nazis.

Making Israel's situation worse, however, was the fact that the people no longer feared the Lord. That's when God had enough. Like a father who has been listening to his child kick and scream in a tantrum and suddenly announces, "That's enough!"—all goes quiet. That's what happened in this instance. "The glory of the LORD appeared in the tent of meeting to all the sons of Israel" (v. 10).

The Rebuke of God

Even though God had shown Himself faithful in delivering and sustaining His people, the Israelites rebelled against Him. Enough was enough. The Lord vowed to send a pestilence to destroy the Israelites and offered to start over with a new nation, with Moses at its head (Num. 14:11–12).

Had I been Moses, I would have said, "Great plan, Lord. Sic 'em!" It's a good thing I wasn't standing in Moses's sandals. Moses realized that if God wiped out His people, then the nations would say He was an impotent deity who could not fulfill His promise to His people. The way Moses saw it, God's reputation was on the line (vv. 13–16). So Moses interceded for those stubborn, fearful people. He begged the Lord to forgive them (vv. 17–19).

And the Lord did (vv. 20–21). However, because that generation continually put God to the test, He decreed they would wander in the wilderness for forty years. With the exceptions of Joshua and Caleb, everyone over the age of twenty would be buried in the desert (vv. 22–35).

The Footprints Fear Leaves in Our Lives

All twelve spies returned with the same information. All twelve agreed that the land flowed with milk and honey. All twelve agreed that there were obstacles in the land: fortified cities and terrifying giants. No one disputed those facts. However, there were two very different responses in their reports: ten spies responded with fear, and Joshua and Caleb responded with faith.

Fear is easier than faith. When adrenaline floods your brain, your gut tightens, your palms sweat, and your mouth goes dry. These are the physical reactions to fear. Emotionally, you imagine all kinds of terror and become fearful of venturing out your front door.

Fear leaves footprints in our lives that impact how we relate to God and others—and we find them in Numbers 13 and 14.

Fear Distorts the Size of Our Problems

I read somewhere that a fog covering seven city blocks doesn't contain enough water to fill a glass, but it will stop traffic. In the same way, it doesn't take much fear to fog our thinking and our ability to function. Fear distorts the size of our problems.

That's what happened to the Israelites. I'm sure if you and I were part of that spy network, we would have said to

Moses, "Look, there are giants in the land. And they are, well . . . gigantic!" This is what we say to the Lord whenever difficulties block our path and separate us from the blessed life. We look at them and think about what it's going to take to deal with those problems. I've counseled parents whose kids have been strung out on drugs. I've counseled businesspeople whose companies were facing bankruptcy. I've performed funerals for young mothers and fathers whose surviving spouses suddenly found themselves single with a house full of kids. I've performed weddings for couples whose marriages then fell apart. Few of us instinctively respond to these troubles in faith; most respond in fear, letting God know that the mountain before us is impossible to move.

Like a funhouse mirror, fear distorts our perspective, fooling us into believing that the terrifying shapes we see reflect reality. They do not. Were there giants in the promised land? Yes, there were. But giants compared to what—compared to whom? Size is relative. Compared to the Israelites, the giants were huge. Compared to God, the giants were tiny.

The tallest building in the world is Burj Khalifa in Dubai, standing at 2,717 feet. But compared with Mount Everest, which stands at 29,029 feet, Burj Khalifa doesn't even reach the jumping-off point at Katmandu.

Fear always utilizes the wrong standard when it comes to sizing up our problems. If you measure your problems according to your abilities, you're going to be terrified. So you have to overcome the only real giant standing in your path—the giant of fear. You do that by measuring your mountains against God. When you do that, your problems are minimized.

Fear Dismisses the Power of Our God

When we allow fear to fog our thinking, we're saying that God is either incapable or unwilling to take care of us. Think again about the number of times the Israelites had witnessed God's power: the exodus from Egypt, the parting of the Red Sea, the provision of manna in the wilderness, the majestic revelation of Himself on Mount Sinai. Memory and experience should have empowered the Israelites, but it didn't. They weren't being asked to trust in some unknown voice from above; God had promised them that land. Yet the Israelites convinced themselves that the same God who had taken care of them in the past would not do so in the present.

Eight times throughout Scripture we're assured that *nothing* is too hard for God. Check out these verses: Genesis 18:14; Job 42:2; Jeremiah 32:27; Zechariah 8:6; Matthew 19:26; Mark 10:27; and Luke 1:37 and 18:27. I looked carefully into the Hebrew and Greek texts to see what nuances the word "nothing" has to teach us. Do you know what I found? "Nothing" means *nothing*—not a thing; not a part, share, or trace; not anything; in no respect or degree; nada; zilch—is too difficult for God.

The Israelites knew all this intellectually. But they couldn't put it together practically. They let fear rule their hearts. When they said they wouldn't confront the giants, they were rebelling against God. That's how Moses characterized it forty years later when he challenged the new generation not to act like their parents did. "Yet [your parents] were not willing to go up," he said, "but rebelled against the command of the LORD your God" (Deut. 1:26).

To act on our fears is to deny our faith and commit the sin of disobedience. How can fear be anything other than defiance when God has given us all we need to move our mountains—Himself, His Son, His Spirit, His Word, and His people? The next time you are overcome by fear, remember all of God's power is available to you. But also remember: to dwell in fear is to dwell in sin. And the sin of disobedience comes at a high cost.

Fear Discourages Our Fellow Believers

Fear is contagious. In Numbers 13, we see how rapidly fear spread in the children of Israel. The Bible says the ten spies came back with a "bad report" (v. 32; 14:37), and their fear infected the people—not just for a week or a month or a year, but for forty years.

Joshua and Caleb tried to inoculate the people with the promises and power of God, but it was too late. Fear gave way to hysteria until the people were left shivering under the fever of discouragement, defeat, and dismay. And if you live in fear—of what might happen to your loved ones or whether you'll have enough for retirement or what the phone call from your doctor will bring—then you're a carrier of discouragement for others and are living in disobedience to God, who commands us not to fear.

Fear Destroys the Promise of Our Future

Theologian E. Stanley Jones observed, "[Fear is] the sand in the machinery of life; faith is the oil."⁶ Fear brought the nation of Israel to a staggering halt. It paralyzed them, keeping them from moving forward and inheriting the land God had promised them. The same can happen to you and to me. Fear will render us incapable of moving forward in the pursuit of God's plan for our lives. It will blind us to the future.

The Israelites had the vision to see beyond Egypt and the Red Sea, but standing on the precipice of the promised land, they lost that vision; they couldn't see past Kadesh Barnea. Blinded by fear, a whole generation forfeited their future and missed the blessing of God. Fear always leads us away from God's future blessings in our lives.

Faith over Fear

What little faith the Israelites had cultivated since leaving Egypt vanished under the scorching wind of fear. Yet faith is the only thing that can conquer fear. But it has to be *genuine* faith. Contrary to what many believe, faith isn't the hope or wish that God will do what we want Him to do. Many Christians equate faith with positive thinking. They say if we believe hard enough, then God will be forced to heal us, restore our marriage, or secure for us a high-paying job. It's the spiritual version of *The Little Engine That Could*. The mountain looms before us and the grade is steep, and we chug off, repeating to ourselves, "I think God will, I think God will, I think God will." That isn't faith; that's presumption.

Here's what genuine faith looks like: "Faith is the assurance of things hoped for, the conviction of things not seen" (Heb. 11:1). Let me break this down so we get a better picture of authentic faith. First, faith is an *assurance*—that refers to the concrete foundation under a pillar or a building. Second, faith is a *conviction*—that refers to unseen realities, like the promises of God. In other words, *faith is our unshakable belief that God will do what He promises to do.* Therefore, we must act accordingly, without fear.

Faith isn't the hope that God will do what we want Him to do but the assured conviction that God will do what He promises to do. God hasn't promised to restore every marriage, heal every physical affliction, or put a chicken in every pot and a Porsche in every garage. He has promised to lead us, protect us, and bless us if we obey Him in faith.

The Path from Fear to Courage

To make this more practical, especially when our fear overshadows our faith, I want to suggest five things we can do to move the mountain of fear and begin walking the path to courage.

Face Your Fears Honestly

Like weeds kill grass, so fear kills faith as soon as it takes root in your heart. Fear might go dormant every now and again, but it won't die on its own. You have to do battle with it, pulling it up by the roots. Unfortunately, too many Christians, like some homeowners, mow it down and pretend they have a lush, green yard.

You can't run away from your fears, so you might as well face them and name them one by one. Be specific; hold nothing back; leave no fear unidentified. Then take them to the foot of the cross and ask the Lord to give you courage. You might even memorize Psalm 34:4: "I sought the LORD, and He answered me, and delivered me from all my fears."

Acknowledge Your Fears as Sinful

It's not enough simply to ask God for courage; you must also acknowledge that your fears are sinful. Remember, disobedience is rooted in fear. Time and time again, God says, "Fear not." Yet we fear. That's not living by faith in obedience to God's command. That's living by fear in disobedience to God's command. The only thing to do is to come to God and confess our sin of fear. And when we do, we can have assurance that God hears and is gracious to us, as the apostle John said: "If we confess our sins, He is faithful and righteous to forgive us our sins and to cleanse us from all unrighteousness" (1 John 1:9).

Improve Your Relationship with God

This may be difficult to hear, but our level of fear is a direct indicator of our level of intimacy with God. Think of it like your car's gas tank. The more you have of God in the tank, the more faith you have as measured by the gauge in your heart. Conversely, the less you have of God in the tank, the less faith you have as measured by the gauge in your heart.

The fear that dominated the ten spies and the Israelites demonstrated that they had drifted from the Lord. The faith of Joshua and Caleb demonstrated that they had remained close to the Lord. The Bible makes it clear that Joshua and Caleb were filled with the Spirit of God, which is why they thought and acted differently. Godly courage comes by rubbing shoulders with the God of courage.

So, when your life becomes threatening and scary, ask yourself these questions: *Do I see problems from a human perspective—from the bottom of the mountain looking up? Or do I see problems from God's perspective—from the top of the mountain looking down?*

After fruitlessly searching for meaning and purpose apart from God, Solomon ended the book of Ecclesiastes like this:

"The conclusion, when all has been heard, is: fear God and keep His commandments. . . . For God will bring every act to judgment, everything which is hidden, whether it is good or evil" (12:13–14). "Fear God" is another way of saying "be intimate with God and His ways." When you fear God, nothing this sin-saturated world throws at you is frightening. But when you don't fear God, everything this world throws at you is frightening.

If you haven't come to Jesus Christ in faith, then you know nothing of what I'm talking about here. Your life is one scary movie after another. But it doesn't have to be that way. Jesus died on the cross to forgive you of your sins. He rose from the dead to give you a life free of fear and full of faith. If that's the kind of life you'd like to have, then all you need to do is turn to Him in faith, confess your sins, and ask Him to forgive you. That's why He came to earth.

Take God Seriously

Many Christians I encounter talk a good game, but when things get rough, they fold their tent and go home. These believers mean well, but they haven't fully invested themselves in following Christ. Like fine china when company comes to visit, they pick God off a shelf and dust Him off and use Him for special occasions—Sunday mornings, Easter, and Christmas—but He's not for everyday life. Their own wisdom, strength, and power are just fine for Monday through Saturday. But God isn't looking for Sunday saints; He's looking for daily disciples.

If you want to improve your relationship with God and conquer your mountain of fear, then become fully committed to following Jesus. Become a sellout, a Jesus freak, a disciple who carries his or her cross daily (Luke 9:23). Be prepared to do what Peter commanded: "Sanctify Christ as Lord in your hearts, always being ready to make a defense to everyone who asks you to give an account for the hope that is in you" (1 Pet. 3:15). As someone once said, "Get on fire for God, and men will come watch you burn." How bright is your bonfire?

Hold On to God's Promises

The Scripture is filled with promises from God. Like with diamonds, all you need to do is dig them up. The only difference is, these diamonds are already cut and polished. When you place them into the setting of your life, they will transform you into a fearless follower of Christ. Here are a few I've dug up for you already, just to get you started: Deuteronomy 31:6; Psalm 27:1 and 118:6; Proverbs 3:25–26; Isaiah 41:10; and 1 John 4:18.

These verses are the best faith investments you can make if you're facing the mountain of fear. Write them on a sticky note and place them on the mirror when you're getting ready in the morning or on your computer at work. Memorize them and meditate on them throughout the day. When fear attacks, they'll remind you that the beauty of faith sparkles like a diamond.

Fear often catches us unaware. When we least expect it, we get a phone call at three in the morning or we feel a lump that wasn't there yesterday or the boss needs to discuss our future with the firm. Fear can come from a thousand different places and times. But no matter where or when it comes, fear always threatens to drown out faith. Don't let that happen.

When you find yourself staring at the mountain of fear, choose to face your fears head-on and place your life and the lives of your loved ones in the powerful hands of God. There, you'll find the courage you need to conquer your fear and enjoy the blessed life.

SIX

MOVING FROM
BITTERNESS
TO FORGIVENESS

PASTOR GARY INRIG TELLS of a man bitten by a rabid dog before the invention of vaccines. The man's condition was incurable. In time, the disease would attack his brain, and he would die a painful, crazed death. The man's doctor struggled with how he should break the news to the unfortunate man. "Sir, I'm sorry; it is the worst possible outcome we could have imagined. Test results indicate that you have rabies. We will do all we can to make you comfortable. But I cannot give you false hope. There is nothing we can do to cure you. My best advice is that you put your affairs in order as soon as possible."

The infected man was silent for a few moments. Then he said to the doctor, "May I have a pen and some paper?"

"Yes, of course," the doctor replied and got the materials the man needed. The dying man set to work. An hour later, the doctor returned; the man was still hunched over, writing furiously. "I'm glad to see that you're writing out your will with such care," the doctor said. The man looked up from the page and said, "Oh, this isn't my will, Doc. This is a list of all the people I need to bite before I die."[1]

You may have a similar list. You may not have it written down, but you've composed one in your head. Your list includes a brother or sister, a friend or coworker, a parent or grandparent, or maybe a stranger you believe has wronged you in some way. Perhaps you've been the victim of abuse. For others, there are no specific names or faces, just a gnawing bitterness at life, God, or people in general.

We have seen too many times the mass killing of innocent people by those who, while often suffering from mental illness, nurtured a root of bitterness. Its deadly fruit has ripened in places like Sutherland Springs in Texas, Sandy Hook Elementary in Connecticut, on the campus of Virginia Tech, in an Orlando nightclub, and at a country music festival in Las Vegas. What all those shootings had in common was the rabies-like disease of bitterness.

An Assortment of Anger

If you struggle with the mountain of anger, the only sure remedy is to remove it from your life by learning to forgive. But to pull out the poisonous root of bitterness, we must first understand something about anger: there's a form of anger that is *not* sinful as well as a form of anger that *is* sinful.

Sinless Anger

The biblical response to anger is that it's something we should avoid. This is the picture we get from the Old and the New Testaments. For example, Psalm 37:8 says, "Cease from anger and forsake wrath; do not fret; it leads only to evildoing." Solomon observed in Proverbs 29:11, "A fool always loses his temper, but a wise man holds it back."

On the New Testament side, in Galatians 5:20, Paul equated anger with idolatry and witchcraft. He tells us to get rid of fleshly (as opposed to spiritual) works, including "idolatry, sorcery, enmities, *strife*, jealousy, *outbursts of anger*, disputes, dissensions, [and] factions." And James gave us this command: "Everyone must be quick to hear, slow to speak and slow to anger; for the anger of man does not achieve the righteousness of God" (James 1:19–20).

All these passages cast anger negatively, and generally that's how we ought to view anger: as something displeasing to the Lord. But not all anger is sinful. In Ephesians 4:26–27, Paul wrote, "Be angry, and yet do not sin; do not let the sun go down on your anger, and do not give the devil an opportunity." What's going on here? How could Paul say anger is evil in Galatians and not evil in Ephesians? Well, first of all, Paul was quoting David—the same David who instructed us to "cease from anger and forsake wrath" in Psalm 37:8. David also said, "Tremble [with anger] and do not sin" (Ps. 4:4). I know that doesn't clear up the confusion, so let me unpack this a little.

"Paul's admonishment is not *never be angry*," a friend has observed. Rather, "do not let your anger fester into bitterness, which is a sin the devil can use, in the biblical context, to divide the church."[2] For as many years as I've been in the ministry, I've been fortunate that none of the churches I've pastored has split. But some fellow pastors haven't been as fortunate. Sometimes churches split because of theological differences. But more often than not, when a church divides into factions, it's because one group of people becomes disgruntled because the pastor said something they didn't like, or the church's leadership decided to include contemporary worship songs in the service (or traditional hymns in the service), or the church introduced a new initiative that upset the apple carts of the "We've never done it this way before" crowd. Church divisions have been with us almost from the beginning of the church—and a prime reason for those divisions is anger. Organizations have been formed to help settle church disputes, and books have been written about it.

As deadly as bitterness can be to a church, it can be equally deadly to a family. Divorce rates are soaring, not only among citizens in the United States and Europe generally but among believers in the Lord Jesus Christ. Unresolved anger is at the root of the majority of divorces. And in extreme cases, bitterness leads to deadly violence within families. "Anger is like fire," my friend said. "It can be a useful servant or a destructive master."[3] But it must be handled with great care. Someone who knew how to handle it was Jesus Christ.

Many of us know the shortest verse in the Bible is John 11:35: "Jesus wept." However, most of us don't know that Jesus also boiled with fury while standing outside the tomb of His friend Lazarus. We'll look at this in more detail in chapter 10, but He wasn't angry at Lazarus or his sisters or the people who were filled with grief. He was angry at death. That's what John was getting at in the original Greek when he wrote that Jesus was "deeply moved" in John 11:33 and 38.

Death is an enemy—"the last enemy," Paul said (1 Cor. 15:26). It was right for Jesus to be angry at death, since it had taken the life of His friend, just as it was right for Jesus to be angry with the moneychangers who defrauded worshipers and defiled God's temple by turning it into a first-century version of Target or Walmart (John 2:13–16). The difference between being angry and *not* sinning and being angry *and* sinning is having a just cause for our anger. Early church father John Chrysostom wrote, "He that is angry without cause shall be in danger, but he that is angry with cause shall not."[4]

Let's make this practical. Wouldn't it be sinful to do nothing while thieves break into my house, abuse my family, and steal my possessions? Protecting my family is a righteous act. But righteous anger is never demonstrated while asserting our own justice; rather, righteous anger is demonstrated while asserting the justice of others.

Sinful Anger

Sinful anger isn't concerned with justice; it's consumed with vengeance. This is why Paul said, "Do not let the sun go down on your anger" (Eph. 4:26). Don't go to bed with angry thoughts churning in your mind. If you do, before you know it, you will churn your anger into bitterness. Paul says to wipe the slate clean. We might say keep short accounts. Seek forgiveness, and give forgiveness.

This wasn't the easiest lesson for me to learn growing up. My brother Tim and I often got into fights. Sometimes it was his fault; sometimes it was my fault. He had an annoying habit of locking me out of the bathroom that separated our two bedrooms, which made me angry. I had a habit of pulling pranks on him—usually out of anger—which made him angry. But my brother and I needed to learn to let some things go and to ask for forgiveness.

The writer of the book of Hebrews said, "See to it that no one comes short of the grace of God; that no root of bitterness springing up causes trouble, and by it many be defiled" (12:15). In Ephesians, Paul put it like this: "Let all bitterness and wrath and anger and clamor and slander be put away from you, along with all malice" (4:31). Grudges, rages, tantrums, and bitter words are never to be a part of a believer's character. These things are unrighteous and sinful. Unfortunately, you may be among those who can hardly get through the day without someone or something pushing one or more of your buttons—the culture, the economy, politicians, your boss, your coworkers, your spouse, your kids, even your pets. By the time you get home, you're lit up like the Las Vegas strip. Paul was saying, "Dude, cool down. Take a breath. Zip your lip." If you don't, then the seed of bitterness will find rich soil in your soul.

The Bite of Bitterness

Bitterness is an attitude that refuses to forgive an offense. Like a child who grasps a toy and declares, "Mine! Mine! Mine!" so a bitter person holds on to his or her hurts and cries, "Mine! Mine! Mine!"

In the New Testament, the Greek term for "bitter" is *pic*. Sounds like someone who picks at a scab, doesn't it? They pick and pick at their wound, and it never heals. That's a bitter person. The Greek word means "to cut" or "to prick."

We read in Luke 22:62 that Peter "wept bitterly" after his betrayal of Jesus. Tears gushed because Peter's conscience was pricked. He was "cut to the quick." In Acts 8, we're introduced to a man named Simon who tried to buy the power of the Holy Spirit, which, of course, wasn't (and isn't) for sale. The apostle Peter told Simon to repent, because "I see that you are in the gall of bitterness" (v. 23). In other words, Simon was so jealous of the apostles that he became a bitter man with a lacerated soul.

We encounter another lacerated soul named Miss Havisham in Charles Dickens's novel *Great Expectations*. When she was younger, in the prime of her life, Miss Havisham was engaged to be married. On the day of the wedding, dressed in her white gown, she stood at the altar waiting for her groom to arrive for their nine o'clock nuptials. The chapel was filled with family and friends. The wedding cake and feast were spread out for the reception. At ten minutes to nine, a message arrived at the chapel. Miss Havisham's beloved no longer loved her; he loved another and had run away with the other woman.

At that very moment, time stopped. Weeks and months and years passed, but not for Miss Havisham. The clocks in her mansion remained set at ten minutes to nine. In her estate, she sat every day dressed in her wedding gown and veil, now yellowed and tattered with age. For decades, the cake and the food sat just as they were laid out for the celebration that never came. On a web-covered table, what remained of the reception feast now sat rotten and covered in mold. Rodents scurried in and out of the room that was to host the party. Many years later, she said to a visitor, "On this day of the year, long before you were born, this heap of decay

. . . was brought here. It and I have worn away together. The mice have gnawed at it, and sharper teeth than teeth of mice have gnawed at me."[5]

She was right. Something sharp had gnawed at her soul. The teeth of bitterness had cut out all that was good in her life. The blessed life promised by the Lord was left to fester and rot behind the dark shadows of a bitter soul. That, my friend, is what bitterness will do to us.

A Bitter Root, a Bitter Fruit

Bitterness can be defined as anger multiplied by time and attention. That's what we see in the life of Miss Havisham. And it's what we see in the life of Cain, the eldest son of Adam and Eve. Most of us are familiar with Cain's story. Not only was Cain the first baby born on earth, but he was also, after killing his brother Abel, the first murderer in human history. Murder was the bitter fruit of Cain's sin, but the bitter root was nourished in a polluted nature—the same kind of nature that resides in us all.

The Bitter Root: the Sin Nature

In Ephesians 2, Paul pointed out three sources of evil: the world, the flesh, and the devil (vv. 2–3). These three account for all the misery that has happened to humanity. But the world and the flesh would be innocent if not for the devil. Throughout Genesis 1, God pronounced His creation "good" (vv. 4, 10, 12, 18, 21, 25). And humankind He called "very good" (v. 31). But Satan sought to corrupt God's good earth and God's very good people. He couldn't have been more successful.[6]

God had created Adam and Eve free and innocent. They were free to be fruitful and produce a family, free to move about the earth and use its resources, and free to steward God's creation. They were innocent of evil, guilt, and shame (2:25) and of dread (3:8, 10). But by the time Satan was through with them, their freedom had turned into slavery and their innocence into culpability. This dramatic shift was accomplished through five subtle steps when Satan slithered into the garden of Eden.

First, Satan planted a *deception of doubt*. He said to Eve, "Indeed, has God said, 'You shall not eat from any tree of the garden'?" (3:1). God had commanded the man and the woman that they could eat from any tree in the garden but not from the tree of the knowledge of good and evil (2:16–17). But notice how Satan planted a subtle seed of doubt in Eve's mind. He asked whether the command of God was that they *could not* eat from any tree of their choosing. That half-truth began to take root, and she wondered whether God's commands were true and trustworthy. Was God holding out on them?

Second, Eve *twisted the truth*. She made the mistake of conversing with Satan. She answered, "From the fruit of the trees of the garden we may eat; but from the fruit of the tree which is in the middle of the garden, God has said, 'You shall not eat from it or touch it, or you will die'" (3:2–3). Satan's seed was beginning to germinate. Eve couldn't distinguish between half-truths and whole truths. She omitted the word "freely," which was a word of grace spoken by the Lord (2:16). Then she added the phrase "or touch it," which God never prohibited. Finally, she diminished the consequences of disobedience. She said, "or you will die," expressing the possibility of death, but God said, "you will *surely* die," expressing the certainty of death (2:17).

Can we pause here for a moment? Eve wasn't unique in mishandling the Word of God. All of us have from time to time. We've ignored unpleasant things, added something that isn't there, and pretended that the Bible doesn't actually say what it says. And though there are some difficult sayings in the Bible that need careful interpretation, most of the Bible doesn't require a working knowledge of Hebrew or Greek to understand God's message. God neither stammers nor stutters; we just choose to plug our ears and convince ourselves that God said something He didn't say. That's exactly what Eve did. She twisted the truth of what God said to help her justify a decision she was about to make.

Third, Satan *questioned God's goodness*. Satan had a ready reply: "You surely will not die! For God knows that in the day you eat from it your eyes will be opened, and you will be like God, knowing good and evil" (3:4–5). Notice that Satan distorted God's words by denying the truth of God's warning. In a subtle but unmistakable way, Satan was saying to Eve, "God is a liar!" Then he offered her a counterfeit truth: "You don't need God. You can be your own god." This is the original lie—that we are sufficient within ourselves, without God.

Fourth, Eve *succumbed to pride*. Moses, the writer of Genesis, entered here and gave us a commentary: "When the woman saw that the tree was good for food, and that it was a delight to the eyes, and that the tree was desirable to make one wise . . ." (v. 6). The poison seed was coming to fruition. Eve gave way to "the lust of the flesh and the lust of the eyes and the boastful pride of life," which "is not from the Father, but is from the world" (1 John 2:16). By seeing that the tree was good for food, Eve gave in to "the lust of the flesh." By gazing on the tree as pleasurable, Eve gave in to "the lust of the eyes." By contemplating that the tree was the secret of wisdom, Eve gave in to "the pride of life." She thought, *All I need and long for is hanging from the tree. I can just pluck and eat.*

Finally, Eve *denied God's goodness.* Satan's deadly seed was now ripe. "She took from its fruit and ate, and she gave also to her husband with her, and he ate" (Gen. 3:6). Notice that Adam was standing there the whole time, yet he never intervened. Not once did he correct his wife's mischaracterization of God's command; not once did he call out Satan's lies; not once did he dissuade Eve from talking with the serpent or reaching for the fruit; not once did he call on God for protection. Why? The answer is simple: Adam wanted to eat from the fruit of the tree of the knowledge of good and evil as much as his wife did.

Paul made it clear that Eve was deceived into sin. He wrote in 1 Timothy 2:14, "It was not Adam who was deceived, but the woman being deceived, fell into transgression." But Adam fell headlong into sin willingly, eyes wide open. As soon as they tasted the fruit—the one that looked so delicious and delectable—it became a poison in their bodies and souls, and they became bitter.

At that very second, Adam, who represents the headship of humanity, passed down through his spiritual DNA what theologians call the "sin nature," described in Romans 5:12–14. Theologian Charles Ryrie said the sin nature blinds our intellect, causing our thinking to become reprobate and our understanding to become separated from the mind of God.

Our emotions are deranged and defiled, and our wills are enslaved to sin, standing in opposition to God.[7]

This nature was passed on to Adam's and Eve's son Cain. And without submitting himself to God, Cain did what was natural when he didn't get what he wanted.

The Bitter Fruit: Anger and Violence

At a time when there were no ob-gyns or midwives, God helped Eve deliver her firstborn son. She gave him the name Cain, which sounds similar to the Hebrew word for "acquired" (Gen. 4:1). Her second child was also a boy, whom she named Abel, which means "breath" or "vapor" (v. 2). It's the same word translated "vanity" at least thirty-eight times in the book of Ecclesiastes. Warren Wiersbe observed, "Cain's name reminds us that life comes from God, while Abel's name reminds us that life is brief."[8] And as it turned out, Abel's life was brief indeed.

In time, Cain became a farmer while Abel became a shepherd (v. 2). No doubt, Adam and Eve led their children in worship. So when the boys came of age and could worship God on their own, they both brought a sacrifice to the Lord. Cain brought "the fruit of the ground," and Abel brought "the firstlings of his flock and of their fat portion" (vv. 3–4).

Genesis 4:4–5 says, "The Lord had regard for Abel and for his offering; but for Cain and for his offering He had no regard." Why? I've read numerous attempts to answer this question, such as maybe Abel gave joyfully while Cain gave begrudgingly, or maybe Abel's offering was a true sacrifice while Cain merely gave out of his surplus.

As I explained in my book *Not All Roads Lead to Heaven*, many Bible scholars believe that somewhere in the white space between Genesis 4:2 and 4:3, God most likely asked both men for an animal sacrifice as a reminder of the seriousness of humanity's sin and the necessity for a blood offering to cover that sin—an offering that ultimately God Himself would provide. Abel may not have understood the reasons for God's command, but that didn't stop him from obeying. However, Cain decided to ignore God's command and offer what he thought would be an equal, if not better, sacrifice.[9]

The writer of Hebrews offered this insight: "*By faith* Abel offered to God a better sacrifice than Cain" (Heb. 11:4). Unlike his brother Cain, Abel approached God in faith, while Cain approached God in unbelief. So Cain was rejected and walked away stewing over his first sin, the sin of *envy*.

Cain became enraged, seething with anger—that's the Hebrew idea behind the phrase "very angry" (Gen. 4:5). His anger was written all over his face: "his countenance fell" (v. 5), meaning his expression contorted into a scowl, with his brow wrinkled and his eyes narrowed. It was as if bile was building up inside, ready to burst forth at any moment. This was his second sin, the sin of *unrighteous anger*.

But the Lord is gracious. He asked Cain, "Why are you angry? And why has your countenance fallen? If you do well, will not your countenance be lifted up? And if you do not do well, sin is crouching at the door; and its desire is for you, but you must master it" (vv. 6–7). On the surface, this sounds like a rebuke. But the Lord wasn't scolding Cain. The Lord was confronting him in an attempt to elicit a confession of sin, with the hope that he would repent. That's what God meant when He said, "If you do well, will not your countenance be lifted up?"

God told Cain to get rid of his envy and anger because if he didn't, the sin of bitterness was waiting in the next room. Paul wrote in Ephesians 4:27 "not [to] give the devil an opportunity," because he will drag us further into sin. But Cain refused to listen to the Lord. Instead of repenting of his earlier sins, he opened the door to his third sin, *bitterness*.

The day came when the bitter bile was more than Cain could stomach, and he led his brother away, where no one could hear his cries for help, and "rose up against Abel . . . and killed him" (Gen. 4:8). Cain knew what he was doing. He was performing a cold, calculated sin, the sin of *murder*.

The apostle John used Cain as a negative example for believers. He wrote, "For this is the message which you have heard from the beginning, that we should love one another; not as Cain, who was of the evil one and slew his brother. And for what reason did he slay him? Because his deeds were evil, and his brother's were righteous" (1 John 3:11–12).

Cain's envy of his brother's relationship with the Lord led to an uncontrollable anger that he nursed until it grew into bitterness that poisoned his heart and drove him to murder his brother.

The Path from Bitterness to Forgiveness

With these two ideas in mind—the bitter root and the bitter fruit—we are now ready to follow the four steps of transforming the mountain of bitterness into forgiveness.

Step #1: Acknowledge You Have Been Wronged

If another person has truly hurt you—if you've been left at the altar, so to speak—then don't deny or bury it. Inevitably, the hurt will surface, and if left unattended will fester into anger, which then will turn into bitterness.

The more I counsel those who have legitimate hurts, the more I'm convinced that one of the most potent forces in the universe is denial. Over time, people convince themselves that they've forgiven their perpetrator, when in reality all they've done is dull the pain through dismissal. Why do they do this? More times than not, it's because the pain is too great to face. It's easier to push pain aside than it is to stand toe to toe with it. But this isn't the only reason we deny wrongs done to us. We also don't want others—or even ourselves—to come to the conclusion that somehow we deserved what we got. For example, the man who cheats on his wife shouldn't be surprised that she may want to divorce him, nor should he become angry, blaming his wife for supposedly driving him into the arms of another woman.

Obviously, some abuses are so great it's best to seek professional help from a Christian counselor. But whether the hurt is large or small, one thing is true: if you don't acknowledge it, the root of bitterness will rear its ugly head and bite you and others. So, if you want to root out bitterness, do as Joseph did in Egypt when he confronted his brothers about selling him into slavery. "You meant evil against me," he told them (Gen. 50:20). There was no denying it. But God did something wonderful out of all that evil: "but God meant it for good in order to bring about this present result, to preserve many people alive" (v. 20).

Step #2: Assess Your Hurt from God's Perspective

Instead of asking, "Why did this person do this to me?" or "What am I going to do to that person?" ask, "What is

God going to do about what that person did to me?" This isn't a question to ask with an attitude of vengeance, though God might bring you justice. Rather, this is a question to ask so that good comes to you and the other person, and God is glorified.

Next to John 3:16, the most famous verse in the Bible is Romans 8:28: "And we know that God causes all things to work together for good to those who love God, to those who are called according to His purpose." The key term in the verse is "good." Unfortunately, many of us have a shallow understanding of that term. To many of us, "good" means our personal satisfaction and happiness. I hate to be the bearer of bad news, but that's not how God defines "good." In fact, Paul tells us exactly how God defines "good" in the very next verse: "For those whom He foreknew, He also predestined *to become conformed to the image of His Son*, so that He would be the firstborn among many brethren" (v. 29).

We may not know what God is going to do in every situation in which we've been wronged, marginalized, or hurt. But we can always know that God will use those situations to mold us into the image of Christ. And one thing is certain: though Christ was betrayed, beaten, and executed without just cause, never once did He allow bitterness to take root in His heart. Look at how Peter put it: "Christ also suffered for you, leaving you an example for you to follow in His steps, who committed no sin, nor was any deceit found in His mouth; and while being reviled, He did not revile in return; while suffering, He uttered no threats, but kept entrusting Himself to Him who judges righteously; and He Himself bore our sins in His body on the cross, so that we might die to sin and live to righteousness; for by His wounds you were healed" (1 Pet. 2:21–24).

Christ died on the cross, the innocent for the guilty, so we might die to the sin of bitterness and become conformed to the image of Christ.

Step #3: Admit Your Failures and Receive God's Forgiveness

I'm old enough to remember when people paid their bills with checks. Every month, you wrote a check to your utility company, your mortgage company, and your insurance company. You stuffed them in envelopes, placed stamps in the upper righthand corners, and dropped them in the mailbox. Have you ever written a check thinking you had sufficient funds to cover the amount only to get a notice from your bank that the check bounced? Not only did you still owe the original amount on the bill, you also had to pay a fine if the bank covered the bill for you.

There's a spiritual principle here: you can't forgive someone if you have insufficient funds in your spiritual bank account. In other words, you can't forgive if you've never been forgiven. If you have never come to Christ in faith and sought His forgiveness for the sins in your life, you're like Cain, filled with envy, anger, and bitterness. The door to forgiveness is just as available as the door of selfishness and sin. The choice is yours. I pray you will open the door of your heart to Christ and ask Him to forgive you of your sins. Others of you who have opened the door to Christ sometimes let your anger get the better of you. In those cases, you need a good, strong dose of 1 John 1:9.

Whoever you are, and wherever this chapter finds you, admit your failures and receive God's forgiveness.

Step #4: Act on God's Forgiveness by Forgiving

Two of the most difficult passages in the New Testament to put into practice are Ephesians 4:32 and Colossians 3:13. Both of these verses command us to forgive those who have hurt us. If the command is not enough to get us to forgive others, Paul added a stinger to each verse: we are to forgive *because God has forgiven us.* We should never forget that God forgave us when we didn't deserve it.

It doesn't do any good to acknowledge wrongs done to you, assess your hurt from God's perspective, admit your own wrongs, and receive God's forgiveness if you refuse to forgive others. Instead, be like Jesus. Forgive—and you'll discover that the mountain of bitterness will move out of your way to give you a clear view of the blessed life.

SEVEN

MOVING FROM MATERIALISM TO CONTENTMENT

A HYBRID OF SAIL AND STEAM, the *Royal Charter* was one of the fastest ships ever built in the United Kingdom. In October 1859, she was returning from Australia with her hold filled with boxes of gold. But that wasn't the only gold onboard. Of her 377 passengers, many carried gold in their luggage or had sewn gold coins into their clothing.

Captain Thomas Taylor was determined to get his passengers and crew to Liverpool, England, despite threatening seas. Turning his ship north into the Irish Sea, Captain Taylor had to lean her into the strong winds. Forward progress was slow, so he ordered the sails struck and the boilers fired; they would proceed by steam. As the *Royal Charter* came in sight of Holyhead, the skies grew ominous. The ship struggled around the island. Then the hurricane struck and drove the ship backward toward the coast of Anglesey. All efforts to steer proved hopeless. Captain Taylor ordered the anchors dropped to stop their drift as the *Royal Charter* was battered by gale-force winds. Distress signals were sent—to no avail. No rescue ship could be safely launched.

Two hours after dropping anchor, one of the chains snapped. An hour later, the other one did too. The *Royal Charter* was pushed onto a sandbar and stuck fast—twenty-five yards from shore. A large wave drove the ship into the rocks, splintering the hull.

Only forty or so passengers and crew made it ashore alive. Many people drowned because they refused to remove their gold-laden clothing.[1] As one writer said, "Humans have a particularly strong and, at times, irrational obsession with possessions. Every year, car owners are killed or seriously injured in their attempts to stop the theft of their vehicles—a choice that few would make in the cold light of day. It's as if there is a demon in our minds that compels us to fret over the stuff we own, and make risky lifestyle choices in the pursuit of material wealth. I think we are possessed."[2]

Many of us are.

Three False Promises Money Makes

What do you think of when you think about a material-ist? Chances are, the images that flash in your mind are of billionaires driving around in Lamborghinis, vacationing in the French Riviera, or hanging out in their New York penthouses. The one image that doesn't come to mind is of someone going to church. For most people, materialism is the opposite of spirituality. But it's not. The truly materialistic person is a very spiritual person; it's just that he or she has turned material wealth into a spiritual pursuit, which the Bible calls *idolatry*.

This might come as a surprise, but you don't have to be wealthy to be a materialist. You can be dirt-poor and still claim that distinction. Why? Because a materialist isn't made by the amount of stuff owned but rather whether that stuff— great or small—owns you. A materialist refuses to believe that the promises money makes are really just lies.

Money Promises Security

I have a friend who some years back completed a $25 million business deal. After taking care of certain business and personal responsibilities, he deposited $15 million in the bank. Can you imagine what you would do if you suddenly had $15 million at your disposal? You wouldn't have to worry about where your next meal was coming from. You could eat steak and lobster every night if you wanted to. If your kids were in college, you could pay for the whole thing in cash. And work? Unless you just liked to work, you could march into the boss's office and say, "*Hasta la vista*, baby," and retire to Hawaii—or maybe even to the French Riviera.

There's not a person reading this book who hasn't longed for such security. The rich man in Luke 12 who built bigger barns to store larger crops wanted security. He said to himself, "Soul, you have many goods laid up for many years to come; take your ease, eat, drink and be merry" (v. 19). Notice the two things the rich farmer wanted out of life: security for the future ("for many years to come") and a luxurious life ("take your ease . . . be merry").

Many of us may think that those are worthy goals. But according to God, they're not! Look at what Jesus said about the rich farmer: "You fool! This very night your soul is required of you; and now who will own what you have prepared?" (v. 20). King Solomon said something similar: "Thus I hated all the fruit of my labor for which I had labored under the sun, for I must leave it to the man who will come after me. And who knows whether he will be a wise man or a fool? Yet he will have control over all the fruit of my labor for which I have labored by acting wisely under the sun. This too is vanity" (Eccles. 2:18–19).

And Jesus said, "So is the man who stores up treasure for himself, and is not rich toward God" (Luke 12:21).

From 2010 to early 2020, the Permian Basin in West Texas experienced the greatest oil boom in history. But on April 21, 2020, the historic boom turned into a historic bust. On that day, for the first time in history, the price of West Texas intermediate crude went negative, trading at negative $30 a barrel. David Arrington, a Texas millionaire oilman, to keep from crying, placed this humorous message on a sign outside of his downtown Midland office: "Will trade oil for toilet paper."[3]

Like oil futures, money and possessions offer no security for the future. "You do not know what your life will be like tomorrow," James said. "You are just a vapor that appears for a little while and then vanishes away" (James 4:14). One day you will be here; the next day you will be gone—and no amount of money or fancy houses can change that reality. Solomon should have followed his own advice. In Proverbs 23:4–5, he wrote, "Do not weary yourself to gain wealth, cease from your consideration of it. When you set your eyes on it, it is gone. For wealth certainly makes itself wings like an eagle that flies toward the heavens."

Money can be a good and powerful tool. But if we set our affections on it—or on the possessions it can buy—then it ceases to be good; it becomes an idol and replaces God in our hearts. The truth is, money cannot protect you. It cannot protect you from a stranger who steals the affection of your spouse. It cannot protect you from a job loss or a stock market crash that causes your savings or dividends to vanish. It cannot protect you from cancer or some other disease that will take your life.

King Tut was buried in a golden sarcophagus, with a gold necklace and bracelets, surrounded by ivory housewares and richly appointed possessions. But when he was dug up, he was nothing but a mummy. All his possessions were shipped to museums for display or stored in crates in a basement somewhere.

Money Promises Peace

The friend I was telling you about who had the $25 million windfall had been living under a $10 million debt for more than fifteen years. Most of us can't imagine the kind of stress such a debt produces in someone's life. But all of us have been squeezed at least a little bit by debt.

A number of years ago, a television game show called *Debt* aired on the Lifetime channel. The premise of the show was to pit three debt-laden Americans against each other in a *Jeopardy!*-style question-and-answer format. But unlike *Jeopardy!*, dollar values won were shown in the negative, indicating the amount of debt the show would pay off for each contestant. The winner of the game had his or her debt paid off completely, going home with nothing but a feeling of freedom and relief.

This is what lottery winners often initially feel. Yet according to reports, lottery winners are more likely to declare bankruptcy than the average American and find their lives more troublesome. Jack Whittaker, for example, won $312 million in a West Virginia lottery. He told a reporter, "I wish I had torn the ticket up." After he won the lottery, his daughter and granddaughter died from drug overdoses. He was also robbed of $545,000 and said, "I don't like what I've become." Many lottery winners struggle with depression, suicidal thoughts, and family breakdown, including divorce.[4] Solomon, who knew a thing or two about juggling a lot of money, wrote, "When good things increase, those who consume them increase. So what is the advantage to their owners except to look on? The sleep of the working man is pleasant, whether he eats little or much; but the full stomach of the rich man does not allow him to sleep" (Eccles. 5:11–12).

Money Promises Fulfillment

By now we should be getting the idea that all these promises of wealth are nothing more than a bag of hot air. Yet we fall for them all the time. We think, *If only I had more money, then I could build my dream house, drive my dream car, take my dream vacation.* That may be true, but it will never bring ultimate fulfillment. Homes, no matter how beautiful, still get backed-up toilets and peeling paint. Cars, no matter how expensive, still get dings and scratches. And vacations, no matter how exotic, still come to an end.

Material things are like salt water. We thirst for them, but the more we drink, the more we thirst. This is why the apostle Paul warned, "Those who want to get rich fall into temptation and a snare and many foolish and harmful desires which plunge men into ruin and destruction. For the love of money is a root of all sorts of evil, and some by longing for it have wandered away from the faith and pierced themselves with many griefs" (1 Tim. 6:9–10).

Money can promise fulfillment, but it can't deliver.

Three Principles the Bible Teaches about Money

As I've studied the Scripture for biblical principles about money, I've discovered at least three that apply to those who struggle with materialism. I've stated them as contrasts to help you remember them.

Secure Money; Don't Worship Money

Developing a balanced view of money can be difficult. It's easy to love it or loathe it. On the one hand, money persuaded the rich young ruler to reject Christ, deceived the rich farmer into thinking all was well, turned Judas into a turncoat, and blinded the eyes of Ananias and Sapphira to their lies about the Holy Spirit. On the other hand, money built Solomon's temple, where the nation worshiped God, provided the food for the Passover meal at the Last Supper, supported Paul on three missionary journeys, and promoted the spread of the gospel throughout the world.

I can testify to the good that money can do in ministry. If it wasn't for the faithful giving of church members at First Baptist Dallas and donors to Pathway to Victory, we would never have had the opportunity to share the gospel with the million viewers who attended our church virtually on Easter

Sunday 2020, while we were practicing social distancing during the coronavirus shutdown. At least ten thousand people committed their lives to Christ after that Sunday service—all because of those who were faithful with their finances.

Thinking on this delicate balancing act, Bible scholar William Barclay wrote, "Money in itself is neither good nor bad; it is simply dangerous in that the love of it may become bad. With money a man can do much good; and with money he can do much evil."[5] The greatest evil when it comes to money or possessions is idolatry—worshiping money. "No one can serve two masters," Jesus said. "Either you will hate the one and love the other, or you will be devoted to the one and despise the other. You cannot serve both God and money" (Matt. 6:24 NIV).

Jesus wasn't saying that money in and of itself is evil. It's not. But if money takes the place of God in a believer's heart—if you believe that it's the provider of your security, your peace, and your fulfillment—then you're worshiping money. This is why Jesus warned His disciples, "Beware, and be on your guard against every form of greed; for not even when one has an abundance does his life consist of his possessions" (Luke 12:15).

Make sure your life is wrapped up in God, not in wealth— or the desire for wealth. This was Paul's point in Colossians 3:5: "Consider the members of your earthly body as dead to immorality, impurity, passion, evil desire, *and greed, which amounts to idolatry.*"

Save Money; Don't Hoard Money

During the years Solomon was on his quest for meaning, he observed that hoarding is harmful. He wrote, "There is a grievous evil which I have seen under the sun: riches being hoarded by their owner to his hurt" (Eccles. 5:13). I think Henry Baggs would agree with Solomon. When a London newspaper asked its readers for a definition of money, Baggs wrote in and won a prize. "Money," he said, "is an article which may be used as a universal passport to everywhere except Heaven, and a universal provider of everything except happiness."[6]

Nevertheless, the Bible does teach that Christians should save money. *We ought to save money to provide for our future needs.* Solomon advised us to look to nature to observe the wisdom of even the smallest critters. He wrote in Proverbs 6:6–8, "Go to the ant, O sluggard, observe her ways and be wise, which, having no chief, officer or ruler, prepares her food in the summer and gathers her provision in the harvest." Even ants understand that harvest season doesn't last year-round, so they set aside food for the winter. The principle applies to us. Our working years are numbered, so it's wise to invest in a 401(k) or make other provisions for the future.

We ought to save to provide for our families. As life expectancies increase, many working adults find themselves part of the "sandwich generation," stuck between children who depend on them and aging parents who are in need of their assistance. Paul admonished families to provide for their family members. Those who do not provide for their families deny the faith and are "worse than an unbeliever" (1 Tim. 5:8). The context is clear: we're to do whatever is necessary to take care of aging parents and grandparents so they don't become a burden to others. My parents and grandparents didn't live long enough for my siblings or me to assist with their welfare, but I know people who have opened their homes to care for aging parents or paid for nursing care. I admire them for their dedication, and I know most of them couldn't have afforded it without savings.

We ought to save to protect against adversity. Don't misunderstand: our ultimate security isn't in our money, but that doesn't mean we shouldn't be prudent. The Lord wants us to find a balance, and His Word will help us do that. Life has a way of coming at us fast and furious. The Great Depression began after the stock market crashed on Black Tuesday, October 29, 1929. The Great Recession began when the housing market collapsed in 2008. And tens of millions lost their jobs as a result of the COVID-19 pandemic in 2020. Obviously, there were certain warning signs leading to these economic troubles, but when a crisis hits, it hits with ferocious force. Even if we survive severe economic times, we'll be dealing with the question of retirement before we know it. And if we do retire, will our sunset years be beset by ever-increasing medical costs?

We ought to save to provide for ministry concerns. During his third missionary journey, Paul received disturbing news from Corinth. He dispatched a letter of correction to that church and commanded them to "put aside and save" an amount of money every week for the needs of the saints in Jerusalem, who were suffering under a famine (1 Cor. 16:2). This was good and proper for them to do since they, too, were part of God's family. It's also an honorable thing for us to do, so we might be able to minister to our Christian brothers and sisters in need.

Spend Money; Don't Trust Money

Like Proverbs 26:4–5, which is about how to deal with fools, similar proverbs are offered about money. Solomon wrote, "The rich man's wealth is his fortress" (10:15). Then in Proverbs 18:11 he wrote, "A rich man's wealth is his strong city, and like a high wall in his own imagination." The New International Version renders the second half of that verse "they imagine it a wall too high to scale." The key word is *imagination* or *imagine*.

The point Solomon is making in both sayings is that money can't be trusted. For example, money can lead to the illusion that investing in alarm systems, security cameras, and weapons will protect you from those who might want to harm you. It may be wise to invest in those things, but they don't offer ultimate security against those who are intent on robbing your home, regardless of how much you spend.

For as long as I knew my grandfather, he spent money like he was down to his last dime. To say he was frugal is like saying a zebra has stripes. He wasn't miserly, but he kept a close eye on his finances. Over time, he amassed a tidy sum in the bank and had a nice home. Then one day he was served with a notice: a former business partner was suing my grandfather for $35 million. My grandfather's net worth wasn't anywhere near that amount. Suddenly, he realized that everything he had saved and all the possessions he had accumulated offered him very little protection against those who sought to bring him harm.

This is Solomon's point. It's fine to enjoy our money; it's a gift of God. In Deuteronomy 8:18, Moses told the people, "Remember the LORD your God, for it is He who is giving you power to make wealth." Solomon echoed that truth in Proverbs 10:22: "It is the blessing of the LORD that makes rich." But while you're enjoying your money—and the things your money can buy—please don't put your trust in it. It bears repeating: "In the blink of an eye wealth disappears, for it will sprout wings and fly away like an eagle" (Prov. 23:5 NLT). Put your trust instead in the One who blesses you with the ability to earn your income so you can spend some of it on material goods.

The Path from Materialism to Contentment

How much money is enough? According to popular tradition, oil tycoon John D. Rockefeller's answer was simple: "Just a little bit more." If you want to know the secret of contentment, then you need to learn to want what you have. This is the one great overriding lesson the Bible teaches about money.[7]

In 1 Timothy 6, the apostle Paul instructed Timothy about how to handle the delicate situation at that time between believing slaves and believing masters (vv. 1–2). His primary concern was that godliness dominate all relationships. With that in mind, Paul moved on to false teachers, who believed godliness was a means of financial gain (vv. 3–5). This same false doctrine is alive and well today in those who preach a gospel of wealth. In fact, Paul concluded this section without mincing words, calling them "men of depraved mind and deprived of the truth, who suppose that godliness is a means of gain" (v. 5).

Then Paul observed, "Godliness actually is a means of great gain when accompanied by contentment" (v. 6).

Contentment—*autharkeia* in the Greek—is an unusual word because it points to a sense of self-sufficiency as opposed to a lack of desire for things. The Stoics often used *autharkeia* in their writings to imply that people need nothing outside of themselves. But that certainly wasn't what Paul had in mind when he used *autharkeia* in 1 Timothy 6:6. Rather, Paul turned the Stoic idea on its head and declared that contentment, along with godliness, expressed a way of living that makes us independent of outward circumstances but not independent of God.

Our relationship with God isn't transactional. God isn't a benevolent grandfather waiting to indulge our every whim as long as we are good little boys and girls. Rather, He's the Sovereign of the universe who knows and does what's best for us, when it's best. Coupled with contentment, godliness refocuses our glance away from all that glitters (the temporal) to all that glorifies (the eternal). It reminds us that God is sufficient to supply all that we need (Heb. 13:5–6). Therefore, Paul says, godliness isn't about how to get more material stuff; godliness is about how to live a life of faith in Christ, content with whatever we possess.

As pastor of a large downtown church in Dallas, Texas, I've gotten to know my share of "movers and shakers"—the connected, the powerful, and the rich. I've been fortunate to meet wealthy people who are more concerned about their relationship with Christ than they are about their relationship with cash. Each of these individuals would agree that whether they had a lot of money or very little money, as long as they had Christ, they considered themselves rich. That's the kind of godliness and contentment Paul was getting at.

Unfortunately, contentment isn't passed down in our DNA; we have to learn it. Fortunately, we have a good teacher in Paul, who also had to learn contentment (Phil. 4:11).

Contentment comes when we adjust our perspective on life from the temporal to the eternal. Paul said, "For we have brought nothing into the world, so we cannot take anything out of it either" (1 Tim. 6:7). We'll quit striving for more and more when we view life through the lens of eternity. We entered the world empty-handed; we'll leave the world empty-handed. Or in the words of John Stott, "Possessions are only the traveling luggage of time."[8] And when our time is up, we put down our luggage and await a better possession—a glorified body and eternal life with the Lord.

Contentment comes when we learn to lead simple lives— more essentials, fewer extras. I know it's popular these days to become a minimalist and get rid of everything that doesn't "spark joy."[9] But that's not what I'm talking about, and neither was Paul when he wrote, "If we have food and covering, with these we shall be content" (v. 8). The word "covering" includes the idea of both clothes and shelter. Paul's point is this: be content with the necessities of life. This isn't about poverty over riches but simplicity over complexity. Praise God that in His great grace He "richly supplies us with all things to enjoy" (v. 17).

When I think about 1 Timothy 6:8, I'm reminded of the Shaker hymn "'Tis the gift to be simple, 'tis the gift to be free."[10] Fewer things are more freeing than simplicity. In our materialistic and consumer-driven world, the temptation to possess more than we can afford has plunged many people into debt and financial slavery. If we want to learn contentment, we must simplify our lives.

A Warning to Those Who Wish to Get Rich

The lesson of godly contentment flies in the face of worldly wisdom—but of course, many of the lessons the Bible teaches do that. We live in a "more, more, more . . . get, get, get" kind of world. Paul lived in the same kind of world. That's why he followed the lesson of godly contentment in 1 Timothy 6 with a warning in verse 9 to those who wish to get rich: they are standing on hazardous ground. It's as if Paul were putting up a big sign: "DANGER! MINEFIELD!" Paul then rattled off four mines that threaten to blow our spiritual lives apart.

First, those who want to get rich fall into *temptation*, becoming easy prey to hucksters and financial schemes. You might remember the email scam purportedly sent from a Nigerian prince who was trying to smuggle a fortune out of his country, and if you supplied your bank account information, he would share some of the fortune with you. According to one investigation, even a decade after that scam was uncovered as a fraud, the "Nigerian prince" was still taking in over $700,000 a year.[11] Paul didn't know about Nigerian princes or email, but he did know about temptations and the traps those who want to get rich can fall into.

Second, those who wish to get rich fall into a *snare*, trapping themselves in predicaments that result in financial loss and debt. Third, they fall into many *foolish and harmful desires*, selfishly pursuing passions apart from God's will. This idea of "foolish and harmful desires" reminds me of two men I knew at a former church. One man was near bankruptcy and didn't have enough money to provide for his family. He asked the Lord for help, and through a business transaction he became a millionaire. How did he use his money? Instead of making wise investments, he squandered it on frivolous things—a lake house, a country club membership and golf lessons, and hunting trips.

The other man was a friend who had been married ten years to a wonderful Christian woman. They had a nice family, with three children. One day, he met an attractive woman at an industry convention and became smitten with her. Over the course of time, he spent thousands of dollars pursuing this other woman with flowers, candy, jewelry, and out-of-town trips to rendezvous with her. It cost him his marriage. He was a victim of harmful desires.

Finally, Paul said that those who want to get rich are plunged into *ruin and destruction*. Their foolish choice results in idolatry in this life and perhaps judgment in the next life (Mark 8:36). Paul expanded on the idea of apostasy and judgment in 1 Timothy 6:10: "For the love of money is a root of all sorts of evil, and some by longing for it have wandered away from the faith and pierced themselves with many griefs."

Now read this carefully. Paul didn't say that money is *the* root of all kinds of evil but that the *love* of money is *a* root of all kinds of evil. As an object, money itself is amoral. It becomes immoral only when we set our affections on possessing it and the possessions it brings—on loving money in place of God. When that happens, we're in danger of doing evil. The insatiable desire for money is not the only reason for evil in the world, but it's a potent one—and it can lead to idolatry, theft, lying, embezzlement, insider trading, murder, pornography, envy, drug dealing, and addiction, just to name a few.

Proverbs 28:20 says, "He who makes haste to be rich will not go unpunished." According to Paul, believers who replace Jesus Christ with money are spiritual wanderers. They may not look like it when we see them at church, but God knows whether they're being genuine or hypocritical. And believers and nonbelievers alike who achieve a level of wealth can become suspicious of family and friends, wondering if they're looking for a piece of the pie. If they haven't achieved what they want, they become envious of and competitive with those who have. Those who love money have a craving that consumes them until they cry out like the robber baron Jay Gould, "I'm the most miserable devil in the world."[12]

Instructions to Those Who Are Already Rich

The lesson of godly contentment isn't only for those who lust after wealth; it also applies to those who have wealth, even if gained through honest, hard work. Paul told Timothy, "Instruct those who are rich in this present world not to be conceited or to fix their hope on the uncertainty of riches, but on God, who richly supplies us with all things to enjoy. Instruct them to do good, to be rich in good works, to be generous and ready to share, storing up for themselves the treasures of a good foundation for the future, so that they may take hold of that which is life indeed" (1 Tim. 6:17–19).

Paul offered two negative applications and one positive application to those who are wealthy. First, *a contented person is not a conceited person.* The term *conceited* means "high-minded"—proud, snobbish, stuck-up, or self-important. This is the Marie Antoinette attitude of "let them eat cake." It has no place in the Christian life, and those who have means must guard against it. One of the best ways to do that is by remembering that everything you have comes from God the Father. Look at how Paul put it: "Fix [your] hope . . . on

God, who richly supplies us with all things to enjoy" (v. 17). If it weren't for Him, where would you be today?

Another way to guard against conceit is to remember where you came from. Most of those who have wealth weren't born into it. They made their wealth through careful planning, hard work, and the blessings of the Lord. Remember "the rock from which you were hewn and . . . the quarry from which you were dug," Isaiah said (51:1). What was the hole Christ lifted you out of? For Jacob it was deception; for Moses it was murder; for Rahab it was prostitution; for Jephthah it was his illegitimate birth; for Samson it was lust; for Elijah it was depression; for Thomas it was doubt; for Peter it was denial. Remembering where you came from will keep you humble.

Second, *a contented person is not a foolish person.* As the old proverb goes, "A fool and his money are easily parted." Why? One reason is that only fools trust in their money for security. Paul was no fool, and he didn't want wealthy Christians to be either. He told them not to "fix their hope on the uncertainty of riches" (1 Tim. 6:17). It bears repeating that money is uncertain because it can be stolen, lost, or destroyed. And in the final analysis, even if it's secure in a vault somewhere, money brings no lasting satisfaction—certainly not in the areas of life that matter most.

Third, *a contented person is a generous person.* The subtle message of verses 18–19 is to give of yourself in doing good works, which in God's economy entails generosity. Are you a wealthy individual? Give it; don't hoard it. Demonstrate a heart of generosity. Give of your treasure, yes, but also give of your time and your talent. You will be paid back a hundredfold. Besides investing in eternity, which Paul called "storing up . . . treasure . . . for the future," you'll also "take hold of that which is life indeed" (v. 19). You will go beyond the *good life* and enter into the *blessed life*—and that's the greatest investment anyone can make.

A Prayer for Contentment

King Solomon wrote, "He who loves money will not be satisfied with money, nor he who loves abundance with its income" (Eccles. 5:10). Too bad Solomon didn't heed his own wisdom. If he had, he would have become content and found happiness.

A contemporary of Solomon, the wise Agur, however, came to a different conclusion. Perhaps it was because he prayed for contentment. Agur's prayer for contentment is a prayer we should all pray to help us conquer the mountain of materialism: "Give me neither poverty nor riches; feed me with the food that is my portion, that I not be full and deny You and say, 'Who is the LORD?' Or that I not be in want and steal and profane the name of my God" (Prov. 30:8–9).

EIGHT

MOVING FROM LONELINESS TO COMPANIONSHIP

———

IMAGINE THAT YOU'VE AGREED to take part in an experiment. You and a group of people are given a ball and are told to toss it back and forth to one another. Everyone should have an opportunity to catch and throw the ball. Except, unbeknownst to you, the ball is never going to come to you. As the game begins, the ball pops around the group. People are smiling and giggling as different people drop the ball or make a bad throw. And even though the ball hasn't yet come your way, you laugh and smile along with the group, watching it bounce here and there as if you were at a tennis match. After a while, however, you start to get frustrated because the ball still hasn't come to you. You start to reach for the ball that's obviously tossed to another person. You hold out your hands and say, "Throw it to me." No one does. Your smile is now forced as you try to hide your increasing frustration. The rest of the group continues to laugh and rib each other whenever there's a bad toss or a bad catch. But you have lost all fun in the game. It's becoming clear that your exclusion isn't random but purposeful. You stop trying and back away from the group.

Now imagine this isn't a game or an experiment; it's your life. Instead of waiting for a ball to come your way, you're waiting for someone to call, send you a text or email, accept your friend request on Facebook, drop by, or simply speak your name. But your phone never rings or buzzes with a message. Your request is never accepted. No one drops by, and no one remembers your name.

Chuck Swindoll told of an advertisement that was placed in a Kansas newspaper: "I will listen to you talk for 30 minutes without a comment for $5.00." It wasn't a hoax. In time, the person who placed the ad was receiving ten to twenty phone calls a day. "The pang of loneliness was so sharp," Swindoll wrote, "that some were willing to try *anything* for a half hour of companionship."[1]

Those who are facing the mountain of loneliness can relate to the men and women who answered that ad. They long for people to remember their name and spend a few moments with them in real companionship.

All of this begs the question, Would you pay five dollars for someone to listen to you? Do you wish you had a place to go where people know you and are happy to see you? If so, then this chapter is for you, because there is nothing a lonely person wants more than companionship.

Only the Lonely

At no time in the history of the world have we been more connected to one another. With the speed of air travel, you can be in Memphis in the morning and Madrid in the evening. And with the internet and smart devices like your phone or tablet, you can become "friends" on Facebook with just about anyone in the world or express your opinions on any number of topics on Twitter and someone on the other side of the world can respond. It's remarkable, if you think about it.

But it's also ironic, because at no time in the history of the world have we been more disconnected from one another. Reality has become virtual, turning "friends" and "followers" into impersonal avatars on a computer screen. The fact is, loneliness is on the rise. Reporting on findings from Pew Research and Cigna, the *Wall Street Journal* wrote, "Amid our huge, unplanned experiment with social media, new research suggests that many American adolescents are becoming more anxious, depressed and solitary."[2] In particular, the article focused on social media's effect on teenage girls. One young lady, Genevieve, said, "Honestly, sometimes I wish we were living in the 'olden' days, when kids hung out with friends and went on dates. But that isn't what my friends and I do."[3] What do they do? Instead of making real friends, they spend their evenings online collecting "likes" by creating personas for themselves they believe will be more likable than their real selves. In a word, today's teenagers are lonely.

The internet, social media, and smartphones aren't the only culprits in the loneliness epidemic among American teens. But they contribute to a sense of isolation without significant face-to-face interactions. National Public Radio, looking at similar data, reported that our workplace cultures also contribute to increased loneliness—tensions with co-workers and disparities between work-life balance are leading causes. Elena Renken, the author of the article, said, "More than three in five Americans are lonely, with more and more people reporting feeling like they are left out, poorly understood and lacking companionship."[4]

Though it won't make our teenagers—or perhaps anyone reading this chapter right now—feel any less lonely, they (and you) are not alone in being lonely. According to a study by the Centre for Social Justice in the United Kingdom, "As many as 800,000 people in England are chronically lonely and many more experience some degree of loneliness."[5] Of these, only "17 percent of older people interact with family, friends or neighbours less than once a week, while 11 percent do so less than once a month." The study went on to show the link between loneliness and "cardiovascular disease, dementia and depression." And that's not all: "Having two or more close friends reduces the likelihood of poverty by nearly 20 percent," the study found. The epidemic isn't just individual; it's having an adverse effect on society in terms of medical expenditures for mental health and suicide prevention, as well as lost wages in time off or jobs lost. In fact, the United Kingdom even appointed a Minister of Loneliness.[6]

To make matters worse, in the wake of the COVID-19 pandemic, mental health professionals fear that the repercussions of school and business closures, along with the recommended "social distancing"—staying at least six feet apart from other human beings and avoiding touch—could have lasting effects on the mental and physical health of those already struggling with loneliness and isolation.

We were created for companionship. Deprived of lifegiving fellowship, we die a little each day, whether our loneliness comes from *spatial distance*, the isolation we experience when we're geographically separated from our loved ones, like not being able to visit aging parents in nursing homes; or *spiritual distance*, the emptiness we feel when we're drained of purpose, which can lead to anxiety, self-medicating the pain, and even suicide.

Five Types of Loneliness

Spiritual loneliness can be just as acute while standing in a crowded room, sitting in a church pew, or sleeping in a bed next to your spouse. In fact, there are at least five kinds of people who experience such feelings of isolation.

The Unmarried

First, *the unmarried* are often lonely. This isn't always true, of course. But in most cases, God's general plan for men and women—except those with the gift of celibacy—is to find their deepest needs for intimacy met in a marriage that endures a lifetime. Christian singles know that, and they desire for that to happen in their own lives. In the meantime, many of them have told me, they have to wait, and while waiting they come home to an empty house, cook dinner for one, and watch the news or a movie with no one to talk to. Dogs and cats can be fine companions, but it's not the same because they can never fulfill the deeper longings of the human heart for human companionship and intimacy. Adam had a whole zoo, yet the Lord recognized he was lonely. He said, "It is not good for the man to be alone" (Gen. 2:18). So God brought Eve to Adam, and he rejoiced in having someone like himself—"bone of my bones, and flesh of my flesh"—to serve as a complement and companion—"Woman" (v. 23).

The Married

The second group that often suffers from spiritual loneliness are *the married*. Though God's plan for most people is to find a lifelong spouse and live together in intimacy and oneness, marriage isn't a cure for loneliness. Some of the loneliest people in the world are married, just not happily.

When Adam and Eve sinned, their intimacy was corrupted. Their first feelings were guilt and shame; they covered their nakedness (Gen. 3:7). Their next feeling was fear; they hid from God (vv. 8–10). Then they felt isolation. Instead of protecting his wife when God questioned the couple about eating the forbidden fruit, Adam blamed her (vv. 11–12).

The Once Married

Third, and this is usually no surprise, *the once married* know the pangs of loneliness. This is especially true if the marriage was, at least at some point, abundant in companionship and intimate in partnership. This is what God intends for every marriage. But sometimes things go awry. Spouses die, and spouses want divorces.

The death of a spouse is bound to happen to all married couples. And when it does, the links that join two hearts together as one—shared experiences, shared values, shared interests, shared tastes in food and furniture—will be severed. The surviving spouse feels as if a part of his or her own soul has been stripped away, because it has. Unfortunately, no one is completely made whole once that part has been taken. A widowed person might remarry and build another life with another man or woman, but no one can fill the void left by the death of a spouse.

Divorce is another kind of death. It's the death of intimacy and trust in the other person. And it's the death of your dreams for the life you thought you would build with your spouse. If you're not careful, that same deathlike experience can carry over into other relationships—feelings of failure, recrimination, and rejection. Unlike the person who has lost a spouse due to death, the divorced person has to find a way to build a new life out of the chaos left from the old life. For the divorced person, loneliness can come with the sour smell of bitterness.

The Mature

Fourth, *the mature* man or woman—the senior citizen— often finds himself or herself alone. For those with more miles behind them than before them, loneliness can be especially painful. They may have already lost their spouse, and almost certainly have already lost siblings and/or friends. As the years pass, those who remember the old days and can speak their language grow fewer and fewer. They don't want to become a burden to their children, but more times than not, they can no longer care for themselves, leaving their kids with hard decisions to make regarding their welfare.

The Lord commanded the Israelites in Leviticus 19:32, "You shall rise up before the grayheaded and honor the aged." Why? Solomon answered at least part of that question in Proverbs 16:31: "A gray head is a crown of glory; it is found in the way of righteousness." Sadly, in our youth-oriented culture, age isn't honored as it should be. In our culture, gray heads often find themselves obsolete and scorned. And many lonely seniors wonder why they linger on in a life that's no longer fulfilling.

The Miserable

Fifth, *the miserable* suffer alone. Those who live with persistent pain also live with persistent isolation, because that's what pain does. Like a wounded animal, the one who suffers trauma retreats into a shell. I'm not so sure that the old saying "Misery loves company" is true. Sure, the miserable sometimes like to tell others about their misery, but the really miserable—those who are hurting at their core—are rarely talkative. It's been my experience that misery loves being alone, not having to explain the pain or tell the story *one more time*. So these deeply hurting men and women sit in their darkened rooms with their darkened thoughts, doing the best they can to cope with the misery and the isolation that comes with it.

One Is the Loneliest Number

Right about now I'm tempted to joke by saying, "How else can I encourage you today?" But loneliness is no joking matter. And if you have suffered through lonely nights, it's not very comforting to know you're not alone in your loneliness—even though it's true.

Theologian A. W. Tozer observed, "Most of the world's greatest souls have been lonely."[7] This is true in the realm of artistic endeavors; consider Vincent van Gogh or Harper Lee. This is true in the realm of leadership; consider Margaret Thatcher or Frederick Douglass. And this is true in the realm of exploration; consider Ernest Shackleton or Richard Byrd. You could probably add many names to the list of great men and women who were also lonely, whether in business, medicine, law, sports, or whatever the field may be. I could give a long list of those who experience loneliness in ministry. Many names on your list would be foreign to me, as the names on my list would be foreign to you. But there's one list that is probably well known by all of us: the godly, lonely servants of God listed in the Bible.

Three Godly, Lonely Old Testament Leaders

One of the greatest people to ever live was the man whom the Lord talked with "face to face, just as a man speaks to his friend" (Exod. 33:11). Moses was a disgraced Egyptian prince who led a ragged people from slavery into the wilderness for forty years. For all that time, he had to put up with complaints and rebellion. When God selected Moses to lead His people, Moses almost crumbled under the weight of isolation. In Numbers 11, Moses complained, "I alone am not able to carry all this people, because it is too burdensome for me" (v. 14). The Lord brought Moses seventy elders to help, but the feeling of isolation never fully departed. Moses was called to leadership, which required him to turn his back on those who followed, isolating him at the front.

Fast-forward about five centuries, and we're introduced to the man God said was after His own heart (1 Sam. 13:14; Acts 13:22). David was a lowly shepherd. But in time, he rose to be a captain in King Saul's army, and then a captain of a band of renegades. When David became king, he nearly lost his kingdom to a coup d'état hatched by his son. We could point to several psalms that express David's feelings of isolation, but one of the best is Psalm 25: "Turn to me and be gracious to me, for I am lonely and afflicted. The troubles of my heart are enlarged; bring me out of my distresses. Look upon my affliction and my trouble, and forgive all my sins" (vv. 16–18).

Following on the heels of King David came the man known as the weeping prophet, who wrote the greatest dirge in the Bible—the book of Lamentations. Jeremiah preached to people whose hearts were so hard he was thrown into a deep, waterless well and threatened with death (Jer. 38:4–6). His audience refused to listen to his warnings of impending judgment. And when the Babylonian army marched into Jerusalem and set the city ablaze, Jeremiah penned his lament. "How lonely sits the city that was full of people! She has become like a widow who was once great among the nations!" (Lam. 1:1). Referring to himself, Jeremiah wrote, "I am the man who has seen affliction because of the rod of His wrath. He has driven me and made me walk in darkness and not in light" (3:1–2). Later, Jeremiah declared, "The LORD's lovingkindnesses indeed never cease, for His compassions never fail. They are new every morning; great is Your faithfulness" (vv. 22–23). Yet for all his faithfulness as a prophet of God, Jeremiah was a man touched with loneliness.

One Godly, Lonely New Testament Apostle

One of the greatest examples of loneliness invading the life of a godly individual is the apostle Paul at the end of his life.[8] We find him in prison, in the heart of Rome. Paul had been imprisoned before in Rome, chained to guards while under house arrest in AD 60–62. During that time, he wrote four letters: Colossians, Ephesians, Philemon, and

Philippians. He was released and continued his ministry to the church for a few years. But when he was arrested the second time, he was thrown into Rome's infamous prison: the Mamertine—a hole in the ground under the streets of Rome, no better than a sewer. This would be equivalent to being sent to Alcatraz in the 1930s or San Quentin today.

When he wrote 2 Timothy, Paul was awaiting a final trial. Acquittal seemed out of the question, and he knew that because he was a Roman citizen, he wouldn't be crucified; he would be beheaded. The only question was *when*. Paul was eager for his close friend Timothy to hurry to Rome. Paul needed companionship and pleaded with him "to come to me soon" (2 Tim. 4:9). And then in some of the most haunting and chilling words to make their way onto the pages of Scripture, Paul wrote, "Come before winter" (v. 21).

Few things can bring an onslaught of loneliness like winter. Dreary and drab days produce dreary and drab hearts, where everything seems to take longer and more effort to accomplish. The poet George Herbert noted, "Every mile is two in winter."[9] This is what Paul anticipated with the onset of that winter and why he urged Timothy to make haste.

Timothy was ministering in Ephesus at the time. To get to Paul, he faced a four-month journey, and once winter set in, travel would be nearly impossible. If Timothy waited until spring, it would be too late—Paul would be dead.

Prison is a lonely experience. While sitting in that hole in the ground, Paul was separated from his friend Timothy and wanted to see him again. But Paul had also been abandoned by one-time friends. He said, "No one supported me, but all deserted me" (v. 16). Demas, who was a "fellow worker" (Philem. 24) and a part of Paul's inner circle

(Col. 4:14), suddenly bolted. Paul said Demas "loved this present world" (2 Tim. 4:10). Afraid he would be arrested as a Christian, Demas packed his bags and left for home in Thessalonica.

But Demas wasn't the only one who hurt Paul. The apostle said, "Alexander the coppersmith did me much harm" (v. 14). It's possible this Alexander was the speaker mentioned in Acts 19:33 and the Christian heretic mentioned in 1 Timothy 1:20. If that's so, he was probably involved in casting idols but professed faith in Christ during the Ephesian revival (Acts 19:11–20). Alexander may have become a leader in the Ephesian church. But somewhere along the way, he deviated from the truth and began teaching heresy (2 Tim. 2:17–18). Refusing to repent, he was excommunicated by Paul (1 Tim. 1:20).

Alexander may have traveled to Troas, another metalworking center, where he continued spreading lies about the gospel (2 Tim. 4:15) and about Paul. When Paul said Alexander "did me much harm" (v. 14), he used a Greek word that was often used to describe an informant's actions. It could be that Alexander informed on Paul, leading to the apostle's arrest.

This still happens today in countries that are hostile to Christianity. Whether through government infiltration or the threat of imprisonment and/or death, some believers—or so-called believers—will turn in Christian leaders to government authorities. Some of these people are imprisoned, forced to renounce the faith or face execution. Others are threatened with the death of their spouses and children unless they blaspheme Christ or convert to Islam or Hinduism.

Alexander appears to have been one of those kinds of informants. And if he would inform on the apostle, he would certainly inform on Timothy, his former pastor. Therefore, Paul told Timothy, "Be on guard against him" (v. 15).

Paul had been hurt, first by a disloyal coworker and then by a charlatan. Can anything be worse than to be kicked when you're already down? Though Luke remained in Rome and ministered to his friend (v. 11), others, like Timothy, were away. Paul had sent Crescens to Galatia and Titus to Dalmatia (v. 10). And his faithful friend Tychicus was sent back to Ephesus, carrying the very letter that begged Timothy to come before winter. Paul also asked Timothy to pick up John Mark, the man who wrote the second Gospel, and bring him along (v. 11).

But it wasn't just the companionship of close friends that Paul needed. He asked Timothy to stop at Troas and pick up three practical items: "When you come bring the cloak which I left . . . with Carpus, and the books, especially the parchments" (v. 13). Paul was probably in his midsixties at the time and the dampness of the dungeon chilled him to the bone. He probably had only the summer clothes he wore when he was arrested. He had nothing to fight off the bitter cold of that subterranean hole, so he requested his cloak.

The cloak would warm Paul's body, and the books and parchments would warm his heart. The books were probably early drafts of the Gospels, gathered in papyrus scrolls or codices (pages sewn into a book). The parchments were probably writings from the Old Testament, collected on vellum (animal skins) scrolls or codices.

With his friends close—Luke, John Mark, and Timothy—and with his copies of the Scripture, Paul could face the executioner's ax with confidence and courage.

The Path from Loneliness to Companionship

No one is immune to loneliness. It's a disease that afflicts everyone from time to time. But some of us struggle with isolation and despair to a greater degree than others. For many, loneliness is a barren mountain that overshadows every aspect of life. No matter what they do, they can't seem to gather the strength to start the journey to a better, brighter future on the other side of the mountain. If that's you, then let me encourage you with practical actions you can take to conquer the mountain of loneliness and discover the path to companionship.

Acknowledge Your Feelings

It doesn't do any good to force a smile and pretend to be the life of the party. You feel just as lonely inside; you're just now a lonely hypocrite. Pious platitudes and holy hallelujahs won't cut it. Loneliness is real and painful, and the best thing you can do is to acknowledge its reality and pain. To quote A. W. Tozer again, "A certain conventional loyalty may lead some . . . to say brightly, 'Oh, I am never lonely. Christ said, "I will never leave you nor forsake you," and "Lo, I am with you always." How can I be lonely when Jesus is with me?' Now I do not want to reflect on the sincerity of any Christian soul, but this stock testimony is too near to be real. It is obviously what the speaker thinks should be true rather than what he has proved to be true by the test of experience."[10]

God made us for Himself and for each other. At times when we wander away from God, loneliness might rush in to fill the void. At other times, friendships wax and wane.

We know this to be true—what Tozer calls "the test of experience"—so why do we pretend that reality is something different? Loneliness is a human experience. To admit you're human isn't saying that you aren't a follower of Christ or that you're a disappointment to Christ. To admit you're human is to admit you are frail and need the help of a friend, which everyone needs.

Activate Your Friendships

We also need to face the reality that sometimes loneliness is a choice. Perhaps you struggle with *self-image*. You cannot accept yourself as God created you, and you've come to believe no one else will either. If this describes you, you need to learn to look at yourself from God's perspective. What does that mean? Well, it means that God isn't in the business of creating junk. Paul said in Ephesians 2:10, "We are His workmanship, created in Christ Jesus for good works." The first part of that verse implies that every facet of your being—your looks, your abilities, your personality—was ordained by God and given to you to create a unique you.

To see yourself from God's perspective also means to accept the fact that you're the recipient of God's favor and friendship. Think about it—the Creator of the universe wants to have a close friendship with you. He loved you enough that He was willing to lay down His life for you. After all, He said in John 15:13, "Greater love has no one than this, that one lay down his life for his friends."

Perhaps you struggle with *self-love*. One of the greatest barriers to friendship is pride, because there's no room in your heart for loving others when all the space is taken up by love for yourself. One of the by-products of pride is independence—and it's hard to make and maintain friendships when you're as independent as a porcupine. Pricked by your quills, people move away. After a while, you feel the coldness of friendlessness and shiver in loneliness. So you lay down your quills and move toward others. But in time, your independence and pride harden, and you begin to prick others again. And so it goes: needing others, we needle others.

Maybe you struggle with *selfishness*. This is often expressed in terms of busyness. "I'm just too busy for friendships," you say. It's true that friendships take time and effort. But anything worthwhile costs something: time, emotional energy, effort, and sometimes our pride. Paul admonished believers to "do nothing from selfishness . . . but with humility of mind regard one another as more important than yourselves; do not merely look out for your own personal interests, but also for the interests of others" (Phil. 2:3–4). Some people are simply unwilling to pay the price. How about you? What price are you willing to pay for companionship?

I could list other reasons that our feelings of isolation are self-inflicted, such as the inability to accept other people's faults or an unwillingness to forgive other people's mistakes, but you get the idea. Friendship isn't a luxury; it's necessary for our physical, emotional, and spiritual well-being. The magazine *Modern Maturity* ran an article about the need for companionship, saying, "Researchers have determined that participation in formal social networks (church and community groups) is an even more important predictor of mortality than one's health."[11]

Because friendships are essential to conquering loneliness, we ought to strive to create friends. I've identified four kinds of friendships we ought to develop. First, *acquaintances* are those we meet during the daily course of life: at the store, at work, in the neighborhood, at church. Most of these relationships are superficial and will never evolve into anything deeper, and that's fine. But some of these will deepen because all friendships begin here.

Second, *casual friends* are those with whom we socialize or have some sort of consistent contact. We know these folks on a first-name basis. Our conversations with them involve superficial topics like the weather, sports, fashion, the stock market, vacations, or work. Such friendships may last for only months, or they may span a lifetime.

Third, *close friends* are those we share more intimate information with. These people might include neighbors, church members, or work associates with whom we feel camaraderie. Such relationships are characterized by mutual agreement on the basic issues of life and a freedom to discuss personal feelings and concerns. At any time in life we might have anywhere from five to twenty-five close friends.

Finally, *intimate friends* are those we allow into our inner world. A person usually has from one to six intimate friends. These are people with whom we can share our deepest feelings with complete openness. An intimate friend is usually the first person we want to talk with in a crisis. Although the nature of such friendships can change, they most likely endure a lifetime, regardless of geographical distance. Even if you move away from one another and are separated for a period of time, when you're with that person it's like you just pick up where you left off.

When it comes to the loneliness scale, acquaintances and casual friends rarely, if ever, will drive away loneliness; close friends might, but intimate friends always will.

Just a word for men: we tend to stay at the first two levels of friendship. We might venture into the realm of close friendships, but many of us would be hard-pressed to name one intimate friend—and I don't mean your wife. That's not how God designed us. We have to work harder and do better at making and keeping intimate friends. Our lives will be the better for it if we do.

Arouse Your Faith

When loneliness kicks in your door, goes to your fridge, and plops down on your couch, you first should acknowledge the feeling. Second, you should activate your network of friends and invite them over to crowd out loneliness. Third, arouse your faith. Saint Augustine wrote this truth about God a long time ago: "You have made us for yourself, and our heart is restless till it finds rest in you."[12] Like a puzzle piece that fits perfectly to complete a picture, so God has created in every human heart a hole that can be filled only by Him. No one else can fill it—not your spouse, not your children, not your parents, not your friends, not your job, not your education, not your wealth, not your possessions. Only God can fill the void. The most basic kind of loneliness is the loneliness of estrangement from God. And only He is the remedy for such loneliness. If you are suffering from a nagging isolation, then there's a good chance your relationship with God is not as close as it should be. So let's do something about that.

Earlier I quoted from Psalm 25:18. Let's look at that verse again. In a prayer to the Lord, David said, "Look upon my affliction and my trouble, and forgive all my sins." David had been experiencing loneliness. One of the reasons for his loneliness was that he had walked away from the Lord—that's why he asked God to forgive his sins. That's a good place for us to start whenever we feel all alone.

What do you need to confess to God? Get it off your chest and begin to repair your relationship. After confession, commit time to God's Word. Paul, in his prison cell, longed for intimate friends and the comfort that only the Word of God could bring—the books of the New Testament and the parchments of the Old Testament. Psalm 119 says about God's Word, "Your testimonies . . . are my delight; they are my counselors. My soul cleaves to the dust; revive me according to Your word" (vv. 24–25).

To Whom Will You Turn?

Almost fifteen hundred years after Paul penned his letter to Timothy, asking him to come to Rome before winter, the English preacher, reformer, and Bible translator William Tyndale penned a similar lonely letter. Imprisoned in Belgium, Tyndale wrote to the Marquis of Bergen: "I entreat your lordship, and that by the Lord Jesus, that if I must remain here for the winter you would beg the Commissary to be so kind as to send me, from the things of mine which he has, a warm cap; I feel the cold painfully in my head. Also a warmer cloak, for the cloak I have is very thin. He has a woolen shirt of mine, if he will send it. But most of all, my Hebrew Bible, Grammar and Vocabulary, that I may spend my time in that pursuit."[13]

Whenever we, like Tyndale and the apostle Paul, find ourselves in the shadow of the mountain of loneliness, we, too, can conquer this mountain by turning to the companionship of friends and the comforts of God's Word.

NINE

MOVING FROM LUST
TO PURITY

A NUMBER OF YEARS AGO, a leather company ran a commercial featuring the 1950s doo-wop group The Five Satins' song "In the Still of the Night." The commercial depicts an attractive woman, on a business trip, walking into a hotel bar. She sits down close to a good-looking man and begins reviewing work. They exchange glances. He's sure she's giving him *the* look. He smiles, gets up, and walks over to her. Without a word, he leans over and drops off his room key and walks out of the bar. Shortly afterward, she puts her papers away and puts on a leather jacket—the product being advertised in the commercial—and picks up the room key. As she leaves, she slides the key over to a rather dumpy-looking middle-aged man sitting at the end of the bar and gives him *the* look. The scene cuts to the company's name and tagline, followed by both men in the hotel elevator. Just as the elevator door closes, the good-looking man does a double take as he realizes the older man holds his room key.

I don't know whether this commercial increased the sale of leather jackets for this particular company, but I do know this: it stuck to a tried-and-true strategy to capture attention. Clearly the executives of this company bought the idea that sex sells. And it does. Christian thinker Peter Kreeft observed, "If lust ceased tomorrow, we would be plunged into the greatest economic depression in history. Remove sex appeal from advertising, advertising from the economy, and the economy from our civilization and what would be left?"[1]

Solomon said, "That which has been is that which will be, and that which has been done is that which will be done. So there is nothing new under the sun" (Eccles. 1:9). There certainly is nothing new about lust; it has been with us almost from the very beginning and will remain with us until the very end—ruining something God created as good and holy.

Lust is an intense, consuming desire for something to satisfy our selfish passions without concern for the well-being of others or the commands of God. The mountain of lust can take many forms, such as the lust for power, the lust for money, or even the lust for food, to name a few. In the Bible, the Greek word for "lust," *epithumia*, is translated various ways, such as "coveting" (Rom. 7:8) or "desires" (Gal. 5:24). But by far the most common understanding of the mountain of lust is what 1 Thessalonians 4:5 calls "lustful passion"— the lust for illicit sex.

As we'll see in this chapter, some sins incur greater consequences than others. Sexual sin is one of those. Like gluttony, lust will whet your appetite but will never gratify your appetite—only purity can do that.

The Most Unique Thing in the World

Sex has become ubiquitous in our sex-obsessed and sex-saturated society, splattered across our movie, television, and computer screens. Nevertheless, it remains the most unique thing in the world.

Creating Image Bearers

The uniqueness of sex is spelled out in the very first pages of the Bible. After God created the earth and filled it with plants and fish and beasts and birds, He said, "Let Us make man in Our image, according to Our likeness; and let them rule over the fish of the sea and over the birds of the sky and over the cattle and over all the earth, and over every creeping thing that creeps on the earth" (Gen. 1:26). The divine act of making men and women in God's image is often referred to by its Latin name: *imago Dei*, which points to the immaterial parts of human beings, including our personality and spirituality.

The implication of being created in God's image is that everyone—male and female, born and unborn, sick and healthy, rich and poor, famous and anonymous, young and old—has been enlivened by the breath of God and therefore possesses inherent dignity and ultimate value. All of humanity has been created in God's image: "male and female He created them" (v. 27). And once God created the first man and woman, His first command to them was to have sex and start a family. After blessing the couple, the Lord said to them, "Be fruitful and multiply, and fill the earth" (v. 28). In other words, reproduce other image bearers—which gets to the heart of why sex is so distinct.

Sex is the only doorway by which the holy God daily enters the world to do the miraculous work that only He can do: create new images of Himself. It's this very uniqueness—this very holiness—that Satan seeks to distort, twist, and turn into sin. And because Satan is a counterfeiter and destroyer, his desire is to take what God intended for pleasure and procreation within the confines of marriage and pervert it into the mundane and ordinary. One way he does this is through the sin of lust.

Two Becoming One

Sex is also unique because it creates oneness out of two. When Moses focused his lens on Adam in Genesis 2, he recorded the Lord as saying, "It is not good for the man to be alone" (v. 18). Adam wasn't physically alone since he lived in a zoo, naming each beast and bird (vv. 19–20), so the Lord must have had something else in mind when He said that it wasn't good for Adam to be alone. What did God mean? The answer is found in the second half of verse 18: "I will make him a helper suitable for him." Adam had companions, but there was no one in the garden specifically suited to meet his need for companionship. That's what the phrase "a helper suitable for him" is getting at. Literally, it means "a helper according to what is in front of him." The idea is that God will create for Adam someone to correspond to him as an equal. Adam was created to rule over the animal kingdom, but not over the helper God would bring to him. This helper will be one-half of a whole, with Adam forming the other half. Think of it like this: the woman will be to the man as the South Pole is to the North Pole, as the right hand is to the left hand, as one puzzle piece is to another puzzle piece.

To fulfill that equal but unique role, God created Eve. "So the Lord God caused a deep sleep to fall upon the man, and he slept; then He took one of his ribs and closed up the flesh at that place. The Lord God fashioned into a woman the rib which He had taken from the man, and brought her to the man" (vv. 21–22). Adam knew he was incomplete, and so was Eve. But when God presented Eve to Adam, he was overjoyed because at last he had a perfect complement. That's the point of the couplets "bone of my bones" and "flesh of my flesh" (v. 23). In a literal way, Eve was made of the same stuff as Adam: human flesh and bone. However, when they came together as bone and flesh, something mysterious happened: two became one—physically, emotionally, and spiritually. Genesis 2:24 says they "become one flesh." This is the unity of sexual intimacy in the bond of marriage.

We can think of this mystery of oneness—of "one flesh"—as two links in a chain. Until they are interlinked, each link is incomplete. But as soon as they're welded together, the links function as a single unit. You can also think about oneness as a rope, woven together out of two independent strands until they are so intertwined they become one. In Ecclesiastes 4:12, Solomon wrote, "A cord of three strands is not quickly torn apart." Applied to Christian marriages, the three strands represent the husband, the wife, and the Lord, bound together in oneness.

The climax of creation ends with this startling sentence: "And the man and his wife were both naked and were not ashamed" (Gen. 2:25). This is the only time in the Old Testament that the word "naked" doesn't entail some form of humiliation. Adam and Eve were physically naked and felt no shame, but they were also emotionally and spiritually naked with each other. There were no secrets, no hidden agendas, no games to play. They were one and inseparable—until Satan entered the picture, and lust followed in his wake.

The Most Distorted Thing in the World

The biblical idea of sex is the joining of one man and one woman in a bond of oneness for one lifetime. Its purpose is pleasure *and* procreation. Anything outside these bounds is out of bounds: adultery, incest, premarital sex, homosexuality, bestiality, transgenderism, pornography, polygamy, polyamory, and anything else you can think of or will be thought of in the future. In Romans 1, Paul used seven adjectives to describe aberrant sexual behaviors. He said they were ungodly, unrighteous, impure, dishonoring, degrading, indecent, and depraved. Underlying all of them is the sin of lust. Because people refused to worship and obey God, Paul said, "God gave them over in the lusts of their hearts to impurity, so that their bodies would be dishonored among them" (v. 24).

The Greek word for "lust," *epithumia*, is morally neutral. It means "desire," "longing," or "craving." Besides the Lord, Amy, and my family, I have three great loves: popcorn, Diet Coke, and Häagen-Dazs ice cream. Whenever I'm watching a movie, I crave popcorn and a Diet Coke. And when I finish off a nice meal, I often want Häagen-Dazs ice cream. In one sense, you could say I "lust" after these things. But unless I eat or drink to gluttony I haven't sinned, because there's nothing moral or immoral about popcorn, Diet Coke, or Häagen-Dazs ice cream. The moral component of *epithumia* (lust)—whether it's good or evil—is determined by the context. Paul uses *epithumia* in 1 Timothy 3:1: "It is a trustworthy statement: if any man *aspires* to the office of overseer, it is a fine work he desires to do." The context there tells us the meaning is good and right.

Nevertheless, during Jesus's day (and ours), the word *lust* is often used as a euphemism for some form of illicit craving. For example, Jesus used *epithumia* to describe fantasized adultery—a lingering, willful stare for the purpose of sexual arousal. To Jesus, mental adultery is just as sinful as physical adultery, even if it carries fewer consequences. He said in Matthew 5:28, "Everyone who looks at a woman with lust for her has already committed adultery with her in his heart."

As we'll see in a moment, before Samson engaged in an illicit sexual relationship with Delilah, he had already had sex with her in his mind. The same is true of David before he summoned Bathsheba to his bed, or David's son Amnon before he raped Tamar, or Solomon before he filled his palace with seven hundred wives and three hundred concubines. And it's true for every man or woman who has cheated on a spouse, slept together before marriage, or performed other activities that are inappropriate to name.

Christian philosopher J. Budziszewski observed, "Lust isn't sexual desire per se, but disorderly sexual desire. The problem isn't the desire, but the disorder."[2] Could anything represent that distortion more than pornography? One writer who has studied its addictive properties stated, "A scientific consensus is emerging that today's porn is truly a public health menace."[3] What makes pornography so dangerous is that it tangles up our brain's wiring, leading to an addiction just as powerful as those to nicotine, alcohol, and cocaine. But like all addictive things, pornography has diminishing returns. It's not just that you continually need more exposure to get the same hit of dopamine, the pleasure hormone, but that you crave the novel—the new that is surprising and shocking. "Like water following downhill," this writer said, "we are drawn to porn that is increasingly taboo—specifically, more violent and degrading."[4]

Pornography doesn't so much change the way we think. Rather, it changes what we crave. For example, studies show that porn addiction has led to an increase in erectile dysfunction in men of all ages; in feelings of marital dissatisfaction and divorce; in risk aversion, neurosis, and lower altruism; in loneliness, secrecy, shame, depression, and a decrease in intimacy with real people; and in men's negative views of women.[5]

Pornography is a distortion of God's design for sex, which is to be enjoyed by a man and a woman within the covenant of marriage. Pornography is dehumanizing because it distorts the image of God within us by reducing the user to an animal and the used to an object. Pornography creates in us crooked cravings so we no longer desire intimacy with real people but seek stimulation from virtual people made up of desirable body parts. And for this reason, pornography, and the lust that underlines it, is one of the most distorted things in the world.

Warnings against Sexual Immorality

Because lust, at its root, distorts our minds into thinking that we do what is right in our own eyes, apart from God—even to the fulfillment of our most base desires—the Scriptures pronounce stern warnings against sexual immorality.

The Will of God

The first warning concerns the will of God, expressed in 1 Thessalonians 4:1–8. Writing to Christians living in Macedonia, a first-century society of free love, promiscuity, and wife swapping, Paul called the Thessalonian believers to holiness.

Invoking the name of "the Lord Jesus," whom they had received in faith, Paul instructed them how they were to carry out their daily lives in order to "please God" (v. 1). The instruction was clear: God's will for us is "sanctification"—to be set apart from the sinful world and to live a life pleasing to Him. Specifically, God's will is that we "abstain from sexual immorality" (v. 3). The Greek word for "abstain," *apechomai*, means "to keep away from," including *all* forms of sexual activity outside the bounds of marriage. This is a command that requires no interpretation, only obedience in possessing our "own vessel in sanctification and honor" (v. 4). The word "vessel" could refer to our own bodies, in which case the idea is self-discipline (1 Cor. 9:27), or to our own spouses, in which case the idea is fidelity in marriage (Prov. 5:18–19). Regardless of how we interpret "vessel," we are to remain holy and respectable in our sexual practices. Unlike those who don't know God, we're not to be controlled by "lustful passion" that might lead to greater sexual sin (1 Thess. 4:5). If we refuse to obey, then we not only place ourselves under God's discipline but we also place our sexual partner under His discipline by "defraud[ing]" him or her from God's blessing (v. 6).

My first pastoral role was as youth minister at First Baptist Dallas. Since I worked with teenagers, one of the recurring themes was the idea expressed in 1 Thessalonians 4:3. I used to think how hard it was to get teenage boys, particularly, who had access to *Playboy* and other magazines, to commit to a life of purity. Little did I know that I had it easy compared to my son-in-law Ryan, who is now the student pastor at First Baptist Dallas. Today's students can access pornography twenty-four hours a day on their smartphones. It's not just teenage boys who are consuming it; it's also teenage girls. Regardless of who is viewing pornography, it's outside the will of God.

Unity with Christ

The second warning concerns our unity with Christ, as Paul outlined in 1 Corinthians 6:15–20. Paul was writing to believers who lived in a debauched society. In fact, Corinth was the Sin City of the first century.

The sexual sins of the culture had crept into the church and had taken root. The Corinthian church had become so distorted that they tolerated incest (5:1–13) and visits to prostitutes (6:12–20). They believed the Holy Spirit somehow exempted them from sexual purity. Paul reminded them that their individual bodies "are members of Christ," united with Him in spiritual oneness (v. 15). Specifically, Paul was getting at the fact that their bodies didn't belong solely to themselves but to Christ, and if they were married, their bodies also belonged to their spouses. So, if you are a believer, whenever you engage in sexual activity outside marriage, you take what belongs to God—your body (vv. 19–20)—and unlawfully give it to someone else, which is a form of stealing. The result is that you steal from God what rightfully belongs to Him (a body that He redeemed) and from your spouse what rightfully belongs to him or her (a body pledged exclusively in marriage).

As if this wasn't bad enough, Paul warned the Corinthians that since they were members of Christ's body, sexual immorality among believers involved Jesus in their illicit activities. Think about this. Whenever you turn on the computer and watch pornography, Jesus is sitting right beside you. Whenever you meet up with a lover in a hotel, Jesus walks through the door with you. Whenever you look at someone and fantasize about what it would be like to go to bed with him or her, Jesus is reading your mind. So repugnant was the thought to Paul that our lusts involved the Lord that he cried out, "May it never be!" (v. 15).

I recall someone saying, "Sex is a function of the body, like eating, drinking, and sleeping. It's a physical demand that must be satisfied. If you don't satisfy it, you will have all sorts of neuroses." Wrong. Sexual intercourse is not animalistic, the mere joining of two bodies. Whether you have sex with your spouse or with a prostitute, Paul says in verse 16, you are engaged body, soul, and spirit. It's an investment of the emotions and will. Nothing in the human experience between two people is more intimate than sex. That is why the joining of two bodies in sexual union is the making of "one body." In a mysterious way, the "two shall become one" (v. 16). In a similar way, anyone "who joins himself to the Lord is one spirit with Him" (v. 17). Therefore, the oneness of two bodies that is created through sexual intercourse joining in the oneness of spirit to Christ is a serious matter.

No wonder Paul warned the Corinthians to "flee from sexual immorality" (v. 18 NIV). No sin is as directly destructive to the sinner as the sin of sexual immorality. Immoral sexual behavior involves the body as the instrument of sin and cannot be reversed. Other sins such as gluttony or drunkenness involve morally neutral objects, like food and drink. Though the body participates in these things, even to excess, which is destructive, they can be corrected through abstinence—unlike sexual sin. As someone pointed out, "Touch can never be untouched; kiss can never be un-kissed; embrace can never be un-embraced."[6] This is why Paul said, "All other sins a person commits are outside the body, but whoever sins sexually, sins against their own body" (v. 18 NIV), which he explains is a "temple of the Holy Spirit" (v. 19).

Paul concludes by reminding us that we "are not [our] own," but have "been bought with a price"—by the blood of Christ (vv. 19–20). This is why you and I must glorify God in our bodies.

The Original Playboy

In December 1953, Hugh Hefner published the first edition of *Playboy*, a magazine dedicated to hedonism and lust. But Hefner wasn't the original playboy. That distinction goes to Samson. He was born at a time of trouble in Israel. The Philistines persecuted the Israelites, and the Lord chose a barren woman from the tribe of Dan to be the mother of a deliverer. The Lord told her that her son would be a Nazarite—one consecrated to perform a special work for the Lord. He was to abstain from wine and strong drink, to let his hair grow uncut, and to avoid all dead bodies (Num. 6:1–8; Judg. 13:1–5).

In his lifetime, Samson would adhere to only one of these commands: he didn't cut his hair. Nevertheless, the Lord was with him (vv. 24–25). In time, "Samson went down to Timnah" (14:1). The phrase "went down" is the first in a series of downward markers pointing to how Samson moved further and further away from the Lord and further and further into lust (14:5, 7, 19; 15:8, 11).

His first recorded words were, "I saw a woman." Then he told his mother and father, "Get her for me as a wife" (14:2). This tells us a lot about Samson's character. First, he was driven by his senses, his passions. He saw a beautiful woman and wanted her. But what his eyes saw blinded him to what his eyes couldn't see: his duty to serve God as Israel's judge. Second, he was headstrong in demanding of his father. Jewish fathers arranged marriages for their sons; sons didn't pick their own brides. Third, he was careless about God's commands. God had made it clear that the Israelites were not to marry Philistines (Deut. 7:3). Yet the woman Samson wanted was "one of the daughters of the Philistines" (Judg. 14:1–2). In desiring to marry a woman who came from an uncircumcised culture, Samson, a circumcised man, showed that his distinction as an Israelite and a Nazirite was secondary to his own wishes and wants.

All three of these characteristics are true of everyone who struggles with lust. They're driven by their passions, not reason; they won't be deterred from satisfying their cravings; and they give little thought to the commands of God.

Samson's parents tried to talk him out of marrying this Philistine woman, but he was determined to have his way. "Get her for me, for she looks good to me," he told them (v. 3). Literally, he said, "she is right in my eyes." The Hebrew word for "right," *yasar*, typically carries with it a meaning of moral good—"upright." But in the mouth of Samson, the word is emptied of its moral content and is reduced to "desirable" or "attractive." He is making a judgment not on the woman's character but on her outward appearance.

Marriage expert Tim Kimmel told the story of Dan and Ann in his book *Grace Filled Marriage*. Tim counseled with this couple before they married. One thing that stood out to Tim most was the fact that Dan and Ann complimented each other on their looks—a lot. Tim wrote, "That's fairly normal. But for Dan and Ann, physical appearance was all they focused on. I hoped that they would expand their attention to each other beyond the depth of each other's skin." It didn't work. A few years later, after Dan and Ann married, Tim was invited to the couple's home. Just inside the front door was Dan's office. Upon walking in, Tim saw a full-length picture of Ann—fully nude. Once he got beyond his initial shock, Tim tried to explain to Dan the ramifications of displaying a nude picture of Ann just off the entryway to his home—of what it communicated to their kids and their kids' friends, and about the pressure it put on his wife. Eventually, Tim said, the picture came down, "but not because of our discussion. Because they divorced."[7]

"She is right in my eyes," Samson said, which is ironic because it anticipates the refrain in the disastrous last five chapters of Judges, where everyone does "what is right in his own eyes." Going down to Timnah and marrying a Philistine woman was just the beginning of a downward spiral to moral chaos, not only in the life of Samson but also in the life of Israel.

Samson married this unnamed woman, but it was a tragic marriage, ending in her murder (15:6). He never married again, but that doesn't mean he became celibate—far from it. Toward the end of his judgeship, which lasted twenty years (v. 20), Samson went down to Gaza and "saw a harlot there . . . and went in to her [house]" (16:1). Shortly after the tryst with the Gaza prostitute, he met and "loved a woman . . . whose name was Delilah" (v. 4).

Three women marred Samson's life—Philistine women who should've been off-limits to him. His relationships with these women began in lust; one turned into love. Samson didn't love his wife, whom he saw as an attractive possession. He didn't love the prostitute, whom he saw as an attractive plaything. He did love Delilah, whom he saw as an attractive partner. But she didn't love him, and he didn't see that until it was too late. Three times Delilah asked Samson the secret of his strength—even hinting at his eventual fate: about "how [he] may be bound" (v. 6). Three times he toyed with her, falsely claiming he would be like any other man if secured by seven cords, tied by new ropes, or had his hair woven into a loom (vv. 7–14). Three times that's exactly what happened. And three times the Philistines attacked, but Samson was able to break free and defeat them. Samson was a thrill seeker, as are all who face the mountain of lust.

Exasperated, Delilah questioned whether Samson really loved her and nagged him until his "soul was annoyed to death" (vv. 15–16). He finally told her the real secret of his strength: he had never cut his hair (v. 17). The strong woman of the Sorek valley had now conquered the strong man of Dan. One evening, he fell asleep in her lap and she shaved his head. And when she called in the Philistines, Samson was unable to defeat them. His strength had left him because his Lord had left him (vv. 18–20). It's ironic that the introduction of Samson first referred to his eyes (14:1–2) because at the end of his life he could no longer see—the Philistines had gouged out his eyes (16:21). No longer would his wandering eyes wander.

Samson was a tragic figure, as are all who are caught in the net of lust. In his death he redeemed his life, not because in pulling down the temple of Dagon he killed more Philistines than he did the rest of his life combined, but because he finally called on the name of the Lord (vv. 21–31)—as should all who have had their lives wrecked by the sin of lust.

For Those Who Struggle with Lust

At least three lessons emerge from Samson's story. First, *lust is no respecter of persons*. Even a person set aside from birth to perform a specific task for God can succumb to its temptation. A strong person like Samson, a noble person like David, and a wise person like Solomon all stumbled over the sin of lust. You and I can too. Through television screens it woos us, in glossy magazines it winks at us, and on the internet it welcomes us.

Second, *lust is persistent and pernicious*. Just because you may have moved this mountain once doesn't mean other peaks don't lie ahead. They do. If it can wear down a strong person like Samson, then it can wear you down too. Don't try to do battle with lust, and don't try to reason with it; it will win every time. The basic principle when dealing with lust is to *run*! That's what Joseph did—when his boss's wife tried to seduce him, Joseph "fled, and went outside" (Gen. 39:12). And that's what Paul advised for young Timothy:

"Flee from youthful lusts and pursue righteousness, faith, love and peace, with those who call on the Lord from a pure heart" (2 Tim. 2:22).

Third, *lust is a killer*. Lust killed Samson, it killed David's first child with Bathsheba, and it killed Solomon's love for God. Of all the sins that tempt us, lust, if acted upon, has the potential to kill us too—physically through a sexually transmitted disease, spiritually through a broken relationship with Christ, emotionally through a breach of trust with those we love, and personally through a ruined reputation.

The Path from Lust to Purity

Chances are, you've already given in to lust in some area of your life. Whatever intense desire you may be struggling with, what can you do to conquer the mountain of lust and find your way to purity? The following ABCD pattern offers hope.

Acknowledge Your Sin

Receiving forgiveness starts with facing the truth head-on, with owning up to your behavior and calling it what it is: sin. The Bible outlines three things you must do to fully acknowledge your sin.

First, *confess your sin*. We have this promise from God: "If we confess our sins, He is faithful and righteous to forgive us our sins and to cleanse us from all unrighteousness" (1 John 1:9). The word "confess" comes from the Greek word *homologeo*, meaning "to speak the same thing that another speaks."[8] In other words, confession is agreeing with God that lust is sin and calling it sin.

Second, *cease your sin.* The Bible calls this *repentance.* It's not enough simply to say that lust is sinful. You must also determine to turn away from impurity and practice purity. Proverbs 28:13 says, "He who conceals his transgressions will not prosper, but he who confesses *and forsakes* them will find compassion."

Third, *claim your forgiveness.* Forgiveness is a two-step process. It begins by confessing your sin and calling lust what it really is: *sin.* It ends by ceasing your sin, repenting of lust by refusing to surrender to it any longer. Then—and only then—will the Lord "purify [you] with hyssop" and "wash [you until you are] whiter than snow" (Ps. 51:7).

Break Your Connections

When I was a youth pastor many years ago—well before the invention of the internet—I was counseling a young man who struggled with lust. I asked him, "When are you most prone to have lustful thoughts?" Without skipping a beat, he said, "When I'm looking at *Playboy.*" I laughed. Anyone looking at pornography will invite lust; it's kind of a given.

One time, while still ministering to youth, I gave a talk on "How to Avoid Temptation." It was a packed house. I had only four things to say: "Don't pull up. Don't pull down. Don't unbutton. Don't unzip." That was the talk. It might seem simplistic, but years later, I still hear from former students who tell me they have shared those same principles with their children.

Avoid situations that are particularly tempting for you. If you're married, refuse to have any sort of relationship with a member of the opposite sex you're unwilling to tell your spouse about. Reserve your most intimate thoughts for your spouse; they aren't for anyone else. Refrain from meeting alone with members of the opposite sex. Beware of your free time. And whether you're married or not, if you struggle with lust, you ought to avoid being alone on the computer at night. Place blocking and accountability software on all your devices that have access to the internet.

Commit to Your Purity

Hebrews 13:4 is a tough verse: "Marriage is to be held in honor among all, and the marriage bed is to be undefiled; for fornicators and adulterers God will judge." You must maintain the same respect for the institution of marriage and your spouse ten, twenty, fifty, sixty years into your marriage as you did on the day you said, "I do."

An old Arab proverb says marriage begins with a prince kissing an angel and ends with a bald man looking across the table at a fat lady. That's why it takes more than romance and passion to keep a marriage alive. It takes commitment— a commitment that must be renewed yearly, monthly, daily, even hourly. To help you keep your commitment, find someone of the same gender who will hold you accountable and will ask you hard questions. It just might save your life and your marriage.

Don't Give in to Your Guilt

Finding release from the guilt of lust can be painful. Confessing the sin of lust to yourself, the Lord, and potentially others isn't easy to do. But once you have confessed your sin and conquered the mountain of lust, don't let others lock you behind the doors of renewed guilt. Refuse to listen to their voices. Instead, you can be free to pursue a life of purity by listening to the voice of Christ, who says, "Truly, truly, I say to you, everyone who commits sin is the slave of sin. . . . [But] if the Son makes you free, you will be free indeed" (John 8:34, 36).

TEN

MOVING FROM
GRIEF TO ACCEPTANCE

———

A YOUNG NEW YORK ASSEMBLYMAN, surrounded by well-wishers and flashing a toothy grin, stood on the floor of the House and reread the telegram that had just arrived: his wife had given birth to their first child the night before. He was overjoyed, but before leaving for home, he had a few more bills to guide through the legislature.

A few hours later, a second telegram arrived. Still smiling, he began to read it. The sparkle in his eyes suddenly disappeared. His face turned grave. He must hurry home. His mother and wife were both dying—in the same house. He ran to the station and jumped on the first train to New York City, arriving at Grand Central Station at ten thirty that evening. He ran through the fog-covered streets to his home on West 57th Street. Before he arrived, his brother told their sister, "There is a curse on this house. Mother is dying, and Alice is dying too."[1]

The house was as dark as his brother's pronouncement. A single gaslight flickered on the third floor. Rushing upstairs, he found his wife semicomatose. Taking her in his arms and listening to her labored breathing, he pleaded with God to spare his wife's life. At two in the morning, a message came from downstairs: if he wanted to see his mother one last time, he needed to come now. An hour later, his mother died from typhoid fever. Gazing into the lifeless face of his beloved mother, he said to his brother, "There *is* a curse on this house."[2]

Heartbroken, he trudged back upstairs into his bedroom, where his wife lay between life and death. He took her into his arms once again and willed life into her dying body. She held on for twelve more hours, finally succumbing to Bright's disease at two in the afternoon. That evening, February 14, 1884—Valentine's Day—he opened his diary, scrawled a large X on the page, and wrote beneath it: "The light has gone out of my life."[3]

On the day dedicated to the celebration of love, Theodore Roosevelt mourned the loved ones he'd lost. Though he would go on to heroics in the Spanish-American War, serve as governor of New York and then as vice president and president of the United States, remarry, and father five additional children, Roosevelt never fully recovered from the losses he suffered that February day.

All of us who have suffered at the hands of death have felt what Roosevelt felt—that the light has gone out in our lives. I thought the same when I lost my mother and father, who both died in their fifties. When we come to the mountain of grief—whether it's the passing of a loved one, the end of a marriage, infertility or miscarriage, a broken friendship, the death of a dream, or the termination of a career—questions fill our minds, and we wonder whether we'll ever get through the grief and get to a place of acceptance.

Grief is a natural process we must go through after a loss, but if we learn to maintain a biblical perspective, we can keep it from controlling our lives. If you're facing the mountain of grief or know someone who is, then this chapter is for you.

Reactions to Death

Whether it's sudden death, like the kind Roosevelt experienced, or other kinds of loss, such as the death of a marriage or the death of a dream, grief hits each of us differently, because we're individuals who deal with death in different ways. However, there are three general reactions to death that seem to be common to most people.

We Deny Death

The most unrealistic response to death is to deny it, to pretend it has no effect on your life. Those who deny their loss simply refuse to believe what they know is true. For example, they don't talk about death. In fact, they just remove the word from their vocabulary. They look the other way. Like ostriches, they hide their heads in the sand and their minds in diversions.

Theodore Roosevelt looked death in the eye many times in his life—when he was charging up San Juan Hill during the Spanish-American War, when he looked down the barrel of an assassin's pistol while running for president in 1912, and when he contracted malaria while exploring a tributary of the Amazon River. But when it came to the death of his cherished wife, he couldn't deal with it. Though he named his daughter Alice, in honor of his wife, he never mentioned his wife's name in his autobiography—it was too painful to recall.

We Laugh at Death

Some people deny death, but others laugh at it. To make a joke out of death keeps it at a safe distance, without ever really facing its certainties.

A number of years ago, comedian Woody Allen said, "I don't want to achieve immortality through my work. I want to achieve immortality through not dying. I don't want to live on in the hearts of my countrymen. I would rather live on in my apartment."[4] I'm sympathetic to his wishes. Who doesn't want to keep on living and wish their loved ones would keep on living too? As humorous as the jokes and quips may be, there's nothing funny about death and loss. Those who laugh in its face are simply masking their pain and fear.

We Fear Death

Many of us have heard that people fear public speaking more than they fear death. If that's so, it's only because they think they're more likely to give a speech than they are to die. In reality, most of us can probably get through life without giving a speech, but none of us can get through life without facing death.

I often hear the elderly and the very ill confess to me, "Pastor, I'm afraid to die." That's a natural reaction for anyone getting ready to step across the threshold of death's door.

Winston Churchill once said, "Any man who says he is not afraid of death is a liar."[5] We fear death because we fear the unknown. Will our deaths be painful or peaceful? What really lies on the other side of death? Believers in Jesus Christ have nothing to fear, because death for us means life with Christ. Paul wrote, "We are of good courage, I say, and prefer rather to be absent from the body and to be at home with the Lord" (2 Cor. 5:8). The manner of our death may be unknown, but for those of us who are Christians, our destination after death is very well known: it is to be immediately in the presence of Jesus. And such a comforting truth drives out fear.

Stages of Grief

Grief is like a dark tunnel. If you've experienced grief, then you know that it's disorienting and frightening, and there are times when you wonder whether you'll ever see light again. Rest assured, you will. And though the old normal, before the loss of your loved one, will have to give way to a new normal, without your loved one, your life will begin again. The challenge is to keep going, step by step, through the stages of grief until you find yourself on the other side of the tunnel.

Those who have written about grief usually identify various stages, ranging from five to seven, but the number of stages isn't important. What's important is that we move through them so we can find renewed peace on the other side of death.

Shock

Death, whether sudden or anticipated, carries with it a sense of shock, altering our reality. We may respond to death with uncontrollable emotions, leading to weeping and wailing, but more times than not it leaves us feeling numb. People often mistake this for "holding up well," but chances are the grief-stricken person is *not* holding up well. Their lack of reaction is a sign of shock, like a person who has experienced a physical trauma. Death is a mental and emotional trauma. The British might pride themselves on the ability to keep a stiff upper lip in times of war, but doing that during times of grief can be harmful. Pent-up emotion often brings on sickness, so we should be extremely careful about congratulating someone for "holding up well."

Proverbs 15:13 says, "A joyful heart makes a cheerful face, but when the heart is sad, the spirit is broken." That broken spirit—and the refusal or inability to express brokenness—potentially leads to physical ailments. That's why Proverbs 17:22 says, "A joyful heart is good medicine, but a broken spirit dries up the bones." Solomon observed, "There is an appointed time for everything. And there is a time for every event under heaven—A time to give birth and a time to die. . . . A time to weep and a time to laugh; a time to mourn and a time to dance" (Eccles. 3:1–2, 4). When someone we care about dies, it's a time to weep and mourn, even in our shock.

Despondency

Grief also brings a sense of laziness. This is natural since we often feel numb after a loss, making it difficult to make even simple decisions like what to eat for lunch, to say nothing about making important decisions. The typical response of one caught in the whirlwind of grief to questions large and small is, "I don't care," "Whatever," or "What difference does it make?" Charles Dickens captured the feeling of despondency well when he wrote, "There have been occasions in my later life (I suppose as in most lives) when I have felt for a time as if a thick curtain had fallen on all its interest and romance, to shut me out from anything save dull endurance any more."[6]

If you are caught in the grip of grief, this is the time to be surrounded by people who love you and can help you move through despondency so you can make decisions.

Regression

If the emotional dam hasn't already broken by the time you reach this stage, the emotions that have been swirling within will come out in a flood. The grieving person will often become preoccupied with the deceased, trying to remember every detail about the loved one's face, personality, and character and the time spent with him or her. Grieving people ask, "Why did my loved one have to die? Where was God?" They might become angry and spit out bitter words at the one who died, the medical personnel who treated their loved one, and God. After Job's loss of his children, his business, and his health, he asked, "Why is light given to him who suffers, and life to the bitter of soul?" (Job 3:20).

If you're giving comfort to the grieving, this isn't the time to answer the "why" questions. That time will come only when the grieving family member or friend is able to think rationally. When it does, if the question of "why" comes up again, you might consider some of these answers:

- We live in a fallen world, stained by sin. Death is a by-product of sin, as Paul said in Romans 5:12: "Through one man sin entered into the world, and death through sin, and so death spread to all men, because all sinned."

- God uses trials, suffering, and death to help us focus on our hope of heaven. Believers are not to grieve the loss of loved ones without hope. Those who died in Jesus are with Him, and a day is coming when the Lord will catch up the living to be with Him and their loved ones in heaven (1 Thess. 4:13–18). After the death of my mother, my father told me, "All that matters to me now is living in such a way that I can see your mother again someday." My dad put his treasure in heaven because he realized that heaven was all the more precious because my mother was there.

- God will use our grief to help comfort others in the future. I've counseled people whose spouses have left them. I tell them that a day will come when the Lord will use them to minister to another person who is experiencing a similar loss. That's the promise found in 2 Corinthians 1:3–4: "Blessed be the God and Father of our Lord Jesus Christ, the Father of mercies and God of all comfort, who comforts us in all our affliction so that we will be able to comfort those who are in any affliction with the comfort with which we ourselves are comforted by God." The word "comfort" comes from *fortis*—to fortify—which means "to strengthen."

- Trials, suffering, and grief are a process by which we grow and mature in our faith. The book of 1 Peter was written to those suffering persecution. Peter told them, "In this you greatly rejoice, even though now for a little while, if necessary, you have been distressed by various trials, so that the proof of your faith, being more precious than gold which is perishable, even though tested by fire, may be found to result in praise and glory and honor at the revelation of Jesus Christ" (1 Pet. 1:6–7). By the time Christ comes for us or we go to Him, He wants our faith to be refined like gold.

Adaption

At this final stage, the grieving person is facing reality and coming to an acceptance of his or her loss. A new perspective begins to dawn. The grieving person is still attached to the dead, but their attachment takes on different intensity and meaning.

No one should rush to get to this stage. People heal differently and at different rates. When I fell and broke my arm, it took nearly a year for it to fully heal to the point where I could do the same things with the same strength before I broke it. Obviously, I wanted my arm to heal quicker, but it took time. The same is true for broken hearts and spirits; healing takes time.

David reminds us, "Weeping may last for the night, but a shout of joy comes in the morning" (Ps. 30:5). Take your time, and let it be. Let your heart grieve for as long as it takes. And remember that in your mourning, the morning is coming.

Two Grieving Sisters

Chuck Swindoll wrote, "Close friends don't need an invitation to come to the bedside of a dying loved one."[7] But as we saw in chapter 1, when Jesus was told about the serious sickness of His friend Lazarus, it hardly seemed to register with Him. Jesus loved Lazarus and his sisters, Mary and Martha, yet His reaction to the news was sort of ho-hum. At least that's the way it appeared to the two sisters, who were watching their brother lose the battle for his life. For two long days they waited for the Lord to arrive in their village of Bethany to cure Lazarus. But He didn't come. And when He finally did show up, their brother had been dead for four days (John 11:1–6, 17).

Those days of waiting must have been filled with anxiety and frustration for Mary and Martha, even as other friends came to offer help and comfort (vv. 18–19). As each day passed, the shadow of death grew darker and darker over their beloved brother—and still no Jesus. They were confused. *We thought Jesus loved us* must have crossed their minds. Where was He? What could be more important than the life-threatening illness of His friend? And when their brother died, what could Jesus do then? It was too late. No doubt their heartbreak over the death of Lazarus was mixed with hostility toward Jesus for His failure to help.

There's an important truth in this for all of us: our faith is put to the test whenever we ask the Lord to heal a loved one and He doesn't. Do we still believe God loves us and wants what's best for us? Can we go on with faith for the future, without our loved one, declaring the greatness of our God?

When Martha finally got the news that Jesus was in town, she mustered the strength to go outside to meet Him, leaving Mary in the house to grieve with friends and family (v. 20). Martha said to Jesus, "Lord, if You had been here, my brother would not have died" (v. 21). Her accusation was filled with deep disappointment, a sense of betrayal, and flashes of anger. The unvoiced question was "Where were You when we needed You the most?"

Even after so many years, I still get questions about where God was when terrorists killed more than three thousand innocent people on September 11, 2001. That question is now also asked about the global pandemic of COVID-19 that killed more people in a shorter span of time than any virus we've dealt with in our lifetimes. "Couldn't God have prevented this pandemic?" "Why did my loved one have to catch it and die all alone while others recovered?" "Why didn't God save my loved one?" "Why did this happen to me?" "Where was God?"

Martha was angry with Jesus. His delay was inexcusable. She couldn't understand why He waited so long. She never doubted Jesus's power to heal, but in that moment of grief she doubted His compassion and goodness. She must have thought, *You could have healed my brother. Why did You wait so long?* Well, we know something Martha didn't: Jesus waited "so that the Son of God may be glorified by it" (v. 4).

There's another important truth to consider here: if you're angry with God because He didn't heal or save your loved one from death, it's okay to be angry. Pour it out to God; He can take it. But keep this in mind as you're going through the process of grief: God didn't save your loved one from death *not* because He isn't good and gracious and loving but because He is in the process of glorifying Himself through the death of your loved one. His ways are higher than our ways and His thoughts are higher than our thoughts, Isaiah

55:9 says. What is a mystery to us is perfectly understood by Him—and will be understood by us someday.

Jesus's absence at the critical hour was a mystery to Martha, but she held on to her faith. Once her anger was spent, she said, "Even now I know that whatever You ask of God, God will give You" (John 11:22). She had no idea what Jesus was about to do, but she believed that faith in Jesus meant eternal life. When Jesus said to her, "Your brother will rise again," Martha responded, "I know that he will rise again in the resurrection on the last day" (vv. 23–24).

After confessing her faith in Jesus, Martha went to get Mary (v. 28). Mary fell at Jesus's feet and leveled the same accusation Martha did: "Lord, if You had been here, my brother would not have died" (v. 32). Mary's tears brought tears to Jesus's eyes. He asked where the tomb was, and they took Him to the place where they had laid Lazarus four days earlier. As He approached the tomb, some in the crowd began to comment on Jesus's love for Lazarus while others accused Him of callousness: "Could not this man, who opened the eyes of the blind man, have kept this man also from dying?" (v. 37).

As Jesus stood before the sealed tomb of His friend, He wept (v. 35)—but He also became angry. The Greek word translated "deeply moved" in verses 33 and 38 is *embrimaomai*. The Greek playwright Aeschylus used this word to describe warhorses rearing up on their hind legs and snorting just before charging into battle.[8]

Mingled with Jesus's tears was outrage. As we saw in chapter 6, He wasn't angry at His Father, who made the world good and whole, but at sin, at the evil that broke the world and brought death into it. Death is unnatural; it's an enemy. Life wasn't meant to end in death, and it made Jesus seethe with anger.

But Jesus was about to do something that would turn weeping into celebration and anger into joy. First, He ordered the stone removed (v. 39). Martha couldn't believe her ears: "Lord, by this time there will be a stench, for he has been dead four days" (v. 39). Jesus responded, "Did I not say to you that if you believe, you will see the glory of God?" (v. 40). His words seem directed at the disciples, not the crowd or the grieving sisters, because of what He had told them when He first received word of Lazarus's condition.

Under His insistence, a few members of the crowd rolled the stone away. Then Jesus prayed and called Lazarus to come out. And to the astonishment of everyone present, Lazarus hobbled out of his tomb (vv. 41–44), resulting in the salvation of many, just as Jesus prayed (vv. 42, 45).

Let me point out two more important truths. First, Lazarus was *resuscitated*, not *resurrected*. If he had been resurrected, there wouldn't have been a reason to remove the stone. A resurrected body is a glorified body and has the ability to move through physical barriers, unhindered and unaided (20:19–20). Second, to Jesus, gravesites are just places from which new life springs. Life entered Lazarus's lifeless body so that he walked out alive. For many who witnessed this miracle, life entered their lifeless spirits so they might never die spiritually (11:25–26). Many more who never witnessed this miracle have come to eternal life by reading about how God glorified Jesus by granting renewed life to Lazarus. This is good news for anyone who grieves the loss of a loved one who died in Christ. That's why we need not grieve as those who have no hope, because those who placed faith in Christ before death are now more alive than they were when they were living on earth.

When You're Comforting the Grieving

If someone close to you is going through the grieving process, what comfort can you offer, especially if they start asking questions about God's presence or His will? Here are some things to keep in mind.

Give Answers with a Balance of Heart and Head

When confronted with painful realities and difficult questions, it's tempting to answer with our hearts, not our heads. This is especially true in the face of death. We often say things that are silly and false, like "God needed another angel in heaven." That sounds comforting, but it's wrong. We don't turn into angels when we die, and God certainly doesn't need another one. When you give answers to the grieving, use your heart to ensure your answers are loving and sensitive but use your head to ensure that your answers are truthful, biblical, and Christ-honoring.

Give Answers That Are Truthful, Even If Painful

The biblical ideal when talking with others is to "[speak] the truth in love" (Eph. 4:15). People who are grieving want answers to their questions, but answers aren't always immediately available. Those who grieve don't like to hear that, but they must because they cannot live on false hope. Sometimes answers are revealed, and sometimes they're not. The question for those who mourn is, "Can you still trust God even if you never know why your loved one died?"

Give Answers That Point to the Gospel

When people grieve, we often point them to the book of Job, hoping they (and we) will find answers there. But Job says more about the sovereignty of God than it does about the meaning of loss and grief. Instead, we need to point mourners to the gospel—to the cross and empty tomb of Jesus and to the hope of new life as the only means of finding life-affirming comfort for our sorrowful hearts.

The Path from Grief to Acceptance

Because everyone grieves differently, offering comfort cannot be systematized. Anyone who approaches grief that way sounds more like a robot spitting out preprogrammed platitudes than a compassionate person searching for the right words to say. After spending countless hours with others who have lost loved ones, as well as experiencing loss in my own life and reading widely about grief, I've developed some practical helps for offering comfort to those who grieve. Keep in mind, however, when you're going through these—and especially when you apply them—that this isn't a program. Rather, these are suggestions that have to be wisely administered to specific situations and specific individuals.[9]

If you're reading this chapter after the loss of someone you loved, then these five suggestions will bring comfort in your grief. To help you remember them, I'll use the acrostic GRIEF.

Give Voice to Your Emotions

Sorrow can cast you into a pit of despair, tempting you to "check out" into an attitude of indifference, where you live in a comatose-like existence rather than as a fully engaged human being. Or, if the pit is deep enough, you might be tempted to "check out" for good—to end your life. That's a permanent solution to a temporary problem. Suicide is never the answer. You can avoid both extremes by giving full voice to your emotions.

As we've seen, Jesus is the supreme example of balance—of weeping freely and expressing His anger at the death of His friend Lazarus. Jesus didn't shake His fist at God or curse Him, and neither should you. But like Jesus, vent your emotions openly and fully. It will keep you from sliding into bitterness or depression. Obviously, you can do this on your own through prayer—and you should. But I also encourage you to speak with a Christian friend or counselor. Be sure to choose someone who will keep confidences and will listen with empathy.

Remember Simple Truths and Practices

It's hard to pray when your heart has been ripped from your chest. I understand. But you need to pray, to go to the One who can make you whole. If you can't form the words of a prayer, then pray the Psalms or the book of Lamentations. Once you've prayed, then praise. David, after he cried out "How long, O LORD?" (Ps. 13:1) also sang to the Lord for His gracious bounty (v. 6). Praise lifts your spirit by turning your eyes off yourself and placing them on the Giver of life.

Once you've prayed and praised, claim God's promises from His Word and remind yourself of simple truths. You will find comfort and courage if you do. For example, Matthew 6:34 reminds us, "Do not worry about tomorrow." Philippians 4:6–7 encourages us to turn our worries into worship. And always remember what Jesus told Martha: "I am the resurrection and the life; he who believes in Me will live even if he dies" (John 11:25).

Involve Others in Your Grief

Reach out. Ask for help. You aren't a burden to others. No one is so big that they don't need help. John Donne famously wrote, "No man is an island, entire of itself; every man is a piece of the continent, a part of the main."[10]

Slow, agonizing soul death comes from isolation. But life and health emerge in community. As we saw in chapter 8, the apostle Paul understood this and needed his friends around him as he faced his own death. With deep emotion and urgency, Paul wrote to Timothy, "Make every effort to come to me soon. . . . Only Luke is with me. Pick up Mark and bring him with you, for he is useful to me for service. . . . Make every effort to come before winter" (2 Tim. 4:9, 11, 21).

Don't retreat into a shell of sorrow. Call for help, and call them to come quickly.

Eat, Dress, and Sleep

When we have been shocked by the reality of death, we often forget to take care of our physical needs. Two scenes from Paul's life illustrate the importance of not neglecting our needs. The first occurred when Paul was being transported by ship from Jerusalem to Rome, and a violent storm hit that lasted for weeks. Paul encouraged the terrified crew to eat, saying, "Today is the fourteenth day that you have been constantly watching and going without eating, having taken nothing. Therefore I encourage you to take some food" (Acts 27:33–34). He then took bread, gave thanks, broke it, and ate, as did everyone onboard—and they were encouraged (vv. 35–36).

The second episode was at the end of Paul's life, when he was a prisoner of Rome in a cold dungeon. As we saw in chapter 8, Paul urged Timothy to bring his "cloak . . . and the books, especially the parchments" (2 Tim. 4:13). The winds were turning cold, and Paul needed his cloak to keep his body warm. And he needed his books, especially his copy of the Scriptures, to warm his soul.

Taking care of yourself doesn't deny the reality of your anguish but rather affirms life.

Forgive Others

Often our grief is a result of a natural disaster or the natural process of getting older. But many times, our grief is a direct result of someone else's foolishness or our own. In either case, we must learn to forgive.

Whether the death of our loved one was the result of a murder, a suicide, or the carelessness of someone like a drunk driver, it's easy to become angry and wish for vengeance. But that's not the way of Christ. Scripture is clear: "Vengeance is Mine, I will repay," the Lord says (Rom. 12:19). Furthermore, Jesus said that we are to forgive those who offend us "up to seventy times seven," which was His way of saying that there's no limit on our forgiveness (Matt. 18:22).

Forgiveness doesn't mean sweeping your hurt under the rug or denying that somebody has wronged you. That's not forgiveness; that's foolishness. Forgiveness requires acknowledging that someone has wronged you but then letting go of your right to hurt them for hurting you. Forgiveness isn't given cheaply; it's costly, but it purchases something very rare—freedom. It offers freedom for the offender from the fear of vengeance and freedom for the offended from the ever-consuming desire for revenge.

A Final Word to Those Who Grieve

When it comes to the mountain of grief, we should remember what my friend often tells those who mourn: "God's answer to grief is not a philosophy but a Person, not something but Someone, not a word but *the* Word, not a myth but the Messiah, not commentary but the cross, not human reason but divine resurrection. God's answer is Jesus."[11] Jesus Christ is the only One who can truly comfort your heartache, mend your broken heart, and help you begin walking the path to acceptance.

WITH THE MOUNTAIN
BEHIND YOU

WHEN SOMEONE ASKED MOUNTAINEER George Mallory why he wanted to climb Mount Everest, Mallory famously quipped, "Because it is there." In those four simple words, Mallory was expressing something natural to our human nature—we're curious creatures. The same question could be asked about why we climb trees or cross oceans or rocket to the moon. We want to see what's on the other side of the hill, the other side of the earth, or the other side of the universe.

Mallory's answer also reveals something that's in our DNA: a human hope to conquer nature. From the beginning, God created us to steward His creation (Gen. 1:26, 28–30; 2:5, 15). Unfortunately, our first parents did a poor job of it and instilled something else into our DNA: sin and death. As a result, creation no longer cooperates with us but is instead hostile and dangerous (3:17–19).

People like Mallory seek out dangerous mountains to challenge themselves. None of us, however, sought out the mountains addressed in this book. They seemed to jut unexpectedly into our path and separate us from the life we desire—the blessed life Jesus promised in John 10:10.

In truth, each of these mountains is a result of living in a fallen world—a world corrupted by sin and sadness. And though each of these mountains appears insurmountable while standing at its base, I hope now that you've reached the end of this book, your faith has been strengthened, your perspective has been altered, and you've discovered new ways to conquer your mountain. Remember, as you rely on God and apply the lessons you've learned in this book, you can find the courage to conquer whatever mountains you encounter in life and become invincible! It's the only sure way to reach the blessed life you and God want.

Before you turn this last page, close the cover, and place this book on a shelf or share it with a friend, let me give you one final thought to encourage you. Always remember: the God who "held the oceans in his hand" and "measured off the heavens with his fingers" and "weighed the mountains and hills on a scale" (Isa. 40:12 NLT) is the same God who promises, "I will go before you . . . and level the mountains" (45:2 NLT). And He is the same God who said, "I came that [you] may have life, and have it abundantly" (John 10:10).

So, whenever you encounter another Everest-like mountain in your life, remember those promises. And never forget that even the tallest mountain doesn't look so daunting from God's perspective.

NOTES

Preparing to Conquer Your Mountains

1. The story of Hillary shaking his fist at Mount Everest and saying he would return to conquer the mountain is perhaps apocryphal and is found in various sources with various wording. This version comes from Hazel Plush, *The Telegraph*, July 20, 2016, "'Life's like Mountaineering—Never Look Down': The Wisdom of Sir Edmund Hillary," https://www.telegraph.co.uk/travel/destinations/asia/nepal/articles/quotes-sir-edmund-hillary-first-man-climb-everest/.

2. William Barclay, *The Gospel of Matthew*, vol. 2, The New Daily Study Bible (Louisville: Westminster John Knox, 2001), 195.

3. Mark Batterson, *Double Blessing: How to Get It. How to Give It* (Colorado Springs: Multnomah, 2019), 81.

Chapter 1 Moving from Doubt to Faith

1. To read more about this experience, see Billy Graham, *Just As I Am: The Autobiography of Billy Graham* (New York: HarperCollins, 2018), 139.

2. "The American Colony in Jerusalem: Family Tragedy," The Library of Congress, accessed December 15, 2020, https://www.loc.gov/exhibits/americancolony/amcolony-family.html.

3. "The American Colony in Jerusalem: Family Tragedy."

4. Horatio G. Spafford, "It Is Well with My Soul," 1873, public domain.

5. Frederick Buechner, *Wishful Thinking: A Theological ABC* (New York: Harper & Row, 1973), 20.

6. Bart D. Ehrman, *God's Problem: How the Bible Fails to Answer Our Most Important Question—Why We Suffer* (New York: HarperOne, 2008), 61.

7. C. S. Lewis, *A Grief Observed*, in *The Complete C. S. Lewis Signature Classics* (San Francisco: HarperSanFrancisco, 2002), 444.

8. Josh McDowell, *Evidence That Demands a Verdict: Historical Evidence for the Christian Faith* (Orlando: Campus Crusade for Christ International, 1972); and Lee Strobel, *The Case for Christ: A Journalist's Personal Investigation of the Evidence for Jesus* (Grand Rapids: Zondervan, 1998).

9. I'm indebted to the fine work of David Jeremiah for many of the ideas found in this section. David Jeremiah, *Slaying the Giants in Your Life: You Can Win the Battle and Live Victoriously* (Nashville: Thomas Nelson, 2001), 146–48.

10. Mark Littleton, "Doubt Can Be Good," *HIS* (March 1979), 9.

11. As quoted in C. Bernard Ruffin, *The Twelve: The Lives of the Apostles after Calvary* (Huntington, IN: Our Sunday Visitor Publishing, 1984), 117.

Chapter 2 Moving from Guilt to Repentance

1. John Ortberg, *When the Game Is Over, It All Goes Back in the Box* (Grand Rapids: Zondervan, 2007), 114.

2. See Sarah Bowler, "Bathsheba: Vixen or Victim?" in *Vindicating the Vixens: Revisiting Sexualized, Vilified, and Marginalized Women of the Bible*, ed. Sandra Glahn (Grand Rapids: Kregel Academic, 2017), 87.

3. Bowler, "Bathsheba: Vixen or Victim?"

4. See Psalm 31:10; 32:3; 38:3; 42:10; 102:3, 5.

5. Norman Cousins, *Head First: The Biology of Hope and the Healing Power of the Human Spirit* (New York: Dutton, 1989), 109.

6. William Grimes, "Robert Ebeling, Challenger Engineer Who Warned of Disaster, Dies at 89," *New York Times*, March 25, 2016, https://www.nytimes.com/2016/03/26/science/robert-ebeling-challenger-engineer-who-warned-of-disaster-dies-at-89.html.

7. Frank Minirth and Paul Meyer, *Happiness Is a Choice: The Symptoms, Causes, and Cures of Depression* (Grand Rapids: Baker, 1978), 70.

8. As quoted in R. Kent Hughes, *1001 Great Stories and Quotes* (Wheaton: Tyndale, 1998), 195.

9. Charles Haddon Spurgeon, *The Treasury of David*, vol. 2 (New York: Funk & Wagnalls, 1882), 451.

Chapter 3 Moving from Anxiety to Peace

1. F. Scott Fitzgerald, "F. Scott Fitzgerald to His Daughter 'Pie,' August 8, 1933," as quoted in *Letters of a Nation: A Collection of Extraordinary American Letters*, ed. Andrew Carroll (New York: Broadway Books, 1997), 341–42.

2. Corrie ten Boom, as quoted in Charles R. Swindoll, *Tales of the Tardy Oxcart and 1,501 Other Stories* (Nashville: Word, 1998), 625.

3. Walter Bauer et al., eds., *A Greek-English Lexicon of the New Testament and Other Early Christian Literature*, 2nd rev. ed. (Chicago: University of Chicago Press, 1979), 505.

4. "Facts & Statistics," The Anxiety and Depression Association of America, accessed November 19, 2020, https://adaa.org/about-adaa/press-room/facts-statistics.

5. David Jeremiah, *Slaying the Giants in Your Life: You Can Win the Battle and Live Victoriously* (Nashville: Thomas Nelson, 2001), 56. I'm grateful to David for the idea of these disclaimers, which I adapted from him.

6. Mother Teresa, *The Joy of Loving: A Guide to Daily Living*, comp. Jaya Chalika and Edward Le Joly (New York: Viking Penguin, 1996), 92.

7. Adapted from Robert Jeffress, *Choose Your Attitudes, Change Your Life: How to Make Life's Circumstances Work for You, Not against You* (Dallas: Pathway to Victory), 61–67.

8. William Barclay, *The Gospel of Matthew*, vol. 1, The New Daily Study Bible (Louisville: Westminster John Knox, 2017), 301.

Chapter 4 Moving from Discouragement to Hope

1. Thomas Edison, as quoted in J. L. Elkhorne, "Edison—The Fabulous Drone," *73 Magazine* 46, no. 3 (March 1967): 52.

2. Charles Edison, as quoted in William J. Bennett, *Book of Virtues: A Treasury of Great Moral Stories* (New York: Simon & Schuster, 1993), 412.

3. Bennett, *Book of Virtues*, 412–13.

4. *Merriam-Webster Dictionary*, s.v. "discourage," accessed November 19, 2020, https://www.merriam-webster.com/dictionary/discourage.

5. The most common word for discouragement used in the New Testament is *ekkakeo* (Luke 18:1; 2 Cor. 4:1; Gal. 6:9; Eph. 3:13; 2 Thess. 3:13); there is also *ekluo* (Matt. 9:36) and *athumeo* (Col. 3:21).

6. Thomas Carlyle, as quoted in Philip L. Jones, "Thomas Carlyle," in *The Baptist Review* vol. 3, ed. J. R. Baumes (Cincinnati: J. R. Baumes, 1881), 255.

7. Jones, "Thomas Carlyle."

8. Vince Lombardi, as quoted in David Maraniss, *When Pride Still Mattered: A Life of Vince Lombardi* (New York: Simon & Schuster, 1999), 217.

9. Julia Jeffress Sadler, *Pray Big Things: The Surprising Life God Has for You When You're Bold Enough to Ask* (Grand Rapids: Baker, 2019), 61.

Chapter 5 Moving from Fear to Courage

1. See Robert Jeffress, *Courageous: 10 Strategies for Thriving in a Hostile World* (Grand Rapids: Baker Books, 2020), 17.

2. For the physical, emotional, and spiritual effects of fear, see Jamie Rosenberg, "The Effects of Chronic Fear on a Person's Health," *The American Journal of Managed Care*, November 17, 2017, https://www.ajmc.com/conferences/nei-2017/the-effects-of-chronic-fear-on-a-persons-health.

3. Edith Hamilton, *The Greek Way* (New York: W. W. Norton, 1942), 289.

4. Aleksandr Solzhenitsyn, *In the First Circle*, trans. Harry T. Willetts (New York: Harper Perennial, 2009), 3.

5. Winston S. Churchill, as quoted in *Churchill by Himself: The Definitive Collection of Quotations*, ed. Richard Langworth (New York: PublicAffairs, 2008), 4.

6. E. Stanley Jones, as quoted in "Fashioned for Faith, Not Fear," Bible.org, accessed November 19, 2020, https://bible.org/illustration/fashioned-faith-not-fear.

Chapter 6 Moving from Bitterness to Forgiveness

1. Adapted from Gary Inrig, *The Parables: Understanding What Jesus Meant* (Grand Rapids: Discovery House, 1991), 63.

2. Derrick G. Jeter, "Wretched Are the Angry, Blessed Are the Meek and Makers of Peace," sermon at Coffee House Fellowship, Stonebriar Community Church, Frisco, Texas, May 23, 2010. Much of the material in this section was adapted from Jeter's sermon on anger.

3. Jeter, "Wretched Are the Angry."

4. John Chrysostom, as quoted in Peter Kreeft, *Back to Virtue: Traditional Moral Wisdom for Modern Moral Confusion* (San Francisco: Ignatius, 1992), 134.

5. Charles Dickens, *Great Expectations* (New York: Barnes & Noble, 2005), 87.

6. This section is adapted from Derrick G. Jeter, "Unde Malum? Where on Earth Does Evil Come From?" sermon at Coffee House Fellowship, Stonebriar Community Church, Frisco, Texas, October 4, 2009.

7. Charles C. Ryrie, *Basic Theology* (Chicago: Moody Press, 1999), 252.

8. Warren W. Wiersbe, "Genesis," *The Complete Old Testament in One Volume*, The Wiersbe Bible Commentary (Colorado Springs: David C. Cook, 2007), 31.

9. Robert Jeffress, *Not All Roads Lead to Heaven* (Grand Rapids: Baker Books, 2017), 80–81.

Chapter 7 Moving from Materialism to Contentment

1. Adapted from "Sinking of the Royal Charter," Anglesey History, accessed November 19, 2020, https://www.anglesey-history.co.uk/places/royal-charter/index.html.

2. Bruce Hood, "Do We Possess Our Possessions or Do They Possess Us?" *Aeon*, October 16, 2019, https://aeon.co/ideas/do-we-possess-our-possessions-or-do-they-possess-us.

3. Christian Wallace, "Boomtown Follow-up: The One-Two Punch," chapter 12 (April 30, 2020), Boomtown (podcast), https://podcasts.apple.com/us/podcast/boomtown-follow-up-the-one-two-punch-chapter-12/id1484408677?i=1000473125482.

4. Abigail Hess, "Here's Why Lottery Winners Go Broke," CNBC, August 25, 2017, https://www.cnbc.com/2017/08/25/heres-why-lottery-winners-go-broke.html.

5. William Barclay, *The Letters to Timothy, Titus, and Philemon*, The New Daily Study Bible (Louisville: Westminster John Knox, 2003), 148.

6. Henry E. Baggs, as quoted in *The Spirit of Missions* 57, no. 11 (1892): 430.

7. I am indebted to Derrick G. Jeter for much of the material in this section, which was adapted from "The Gains of Godliness," sermon at Coffee House Fellowship, Stonebriar Community Church, Frisco, Texas, n.d. 2007.

8. John R. W. Stott, *The Message of 1 Timothy & Titus: Guard the Truth* (Downers Grove, IL: InterVarsity, 1996), 150.

9. Marie Kondo, *The Life-Changing Magic of Tidying Up: The Japanese Art of Decluttering and Organizing* (Berkeley, CA: Ten Speed Press, 2014), 39.

10. Joseph Brackett, "Simple Gifts," 1848, public domain.

11. Megan Leonhardt, "'Nigerian Prince' Email Scams Still Rake In over $700,000 a Year—Here's How to Protect Yourself," CNBC Make It, April 18, 2019, https://www.cnbc.com/2019/04/18/nigerian-prince-scams-still-rake-in-over-700000-dollars-a-year.html.

12. Jay Gould, as quoted in Stott, *The Message of 1 Timothy & Titus*, 153.

Chapter 8 Moving from Loneliness to Companionship

1. Charles R. Swindoll, *Killing Giants, Pulling Thorns* (Grand Rapids: Zondervan, 1994), 44–45, emphasis in original.

2. Mary Pipher and Sara Pipher Gilliam, "The Lonely Burden of Today's Teenage Girls," *Wall Street Journal*, August 15, 2019, https://www.wsj.com/articles/the-lonely-burden-of-todays-teenage-girls-11565883328.

3. Pipher and Gilliam, "The Lonely Burden."

4. Elena Renken, "Most Americans Are Lonely, and Our Workplace Culture May Not Be Helping," National Public Radio, January 23, 2020, https://www.npr.org/sections/health-shots/2020/01/23/798676465/most-americans-are-lonely-and-our-workplace-culture-may-not-be-helping.

5. Edward Davies, "Loneliness Is a Modern Scourge, but It Doesn't Have to Be," Centre for Social Justice, as quoted in James K. A. Smith, *On the Road with Saint Augustine: A Real-World Spirituality for Restless Hearts* (Grand Rapids: Brazos, 2019), 128.

6. Davies, "Loneliness Is a Modern Scourge."

7. A. W. Tozer, *Man, the Dwelling Place of God*, BreakoutMinistry.org, accessed November 19, 2020, http://breakoutministry.org/wp-content/uploads/2016/06/Man-the-dwelling-place-of-God-tozer.pdf, 94.

8. Derrick G. Jeter's material from "The Last Request of a Dying Man," sermon at Coffee House Fellowship, Stonebriar Community Church, Frisco, Texas, March 22, 2015, was extremely helpful in this section.

9. George Herbert, *The English Poems of George Herbert, Together with His Collection of Proverbs Entitled Jucla Prudentum* (London: Rivingtons, 1871), 252.

10. Tozer, *Man, the Dwelling Place of God*, 142.

11. *Modern Maturity*, February–March 1990, 18–19, as quoted in Robert Jeffress, *Choose Your Attitude, Change Your Life: How to Make Life's Circumstances Work for You, Not against You* (Dallas: Pathway to Victory, 2019), 178–79.

12. Augustine, *The Confessions*, 1.1.1, trans. Philip Burton (New York: Everyman Library, 2001), 5.

13. William Tyndale, as quoted in Handley C. G. Moule, *The Second Epistle to Timothy*, in John R. W. Stott, *The Message of 2 Timothy: Guard the Gospel*, The Bible Speaks Today (Downers Grove, IL: Inter-Varsity, 1973), 121.

Chapter 9 Moving from Lust to Purity

1. Peter Kreeft, *Back to Virtue: Traditional Moral Wisdom for Modern Moral Confusion* (San Francisco: Ignatius, 1992), 165.

2. J. Budziszewski, *On the Meaning of Sex* (Wilmington, DE: ISI Books, 2012), 112.

3. Pascal-Emmanuel Gobry, "A Science-Based Case for Ending the Porn Epidemic," *American Greatness*, December 15, 2019, https://amgreat ness.com/2019/12/15/a-science-base-case-for-ending-the-porn-epidemic/.

4. Gobry, "A Science-Based Case for Ending the Porn Epidemic."

5. Gobry, "A Science-Based Case for Ending the Porn Epidemic."

6. Derrick G. Jeter, *The Sanctity of Life: The Inescapable Issue Bible Companion* (Frisco, TX: IFL Publishing House, 2015), 41.

7. Tim and Darcy Kimmel, *Grace Filled Marriage* (Franklin, TN: Worthy, 2013), 96–97.

8. Kenneth S. Wuest, *Wuest's Word Studies from the Greek New Testament*, 2nd ed. (Grand Rapids: Eerdmans, 1954), 2:104.

Chapter 10 Moving from Grief to Acceptance

1. Elliot Roosevelt to Corinne Roosevelt, as quoted in Edmund Morris, *The Rise of Theodore Roosevelt* (New York: Coward, McCann & Geoghegan, 1979), 240.

2. As quoted in Morris, *Rise of Theodore Roosevelt*, 241.

3. As quoted in Morris, *Rise of Theodore Roosevelt*, 241.

4. As quoted in Dinesh D'Souza, *Life after Death: The Evidence* (Washington, DC: Regnery, 2009), 4.

5. As quoted in James C. Humes, *The Wit and Wisdom of Winston Churchill* (New York: Harper Perennial, 1995), 25.

6. Charles Dickens, *Great Expectations* (New York: Barnes & Noble, 2005), 104.

7. Charles R. Swindoll, *Getting Through the Tough Stuff* (Nashville: W Publishing, 2004), 212.

8. Aeschylus, "Seven against Thebes," *The Lyric Dramas of Aeschylus*, trans. John Stuart Blackie (repr. London: J. M. Dent, 1911), 275.

9. I'm grateful for the help of Derrick G. Jeter in developing these principles, as well as some of the ideas in this section. His insights are adapted from his sermons "A Soul Drenched in Tears: Why Me and How Do I Endure?" and "A Deeper Mystery: What Do We Say to Those Who Ask?," both originally delivered to Coffee House Fellowship, Stonebriar Community Church, Frisco, Texas, November 8, 2009, and November 15, 2009, respectively.

10. John Donne, "XVII *Nuc Lento Sonitu Dicunt, Morieris*," in *Donne: Poems and Prose* (New York: Everyman's Library, 1995), 227.

11. Jeter, "A Deeper Mystery."

ABOUT THE AUTHOR

Dr. Robert Jeffress is senior pastor of the fourteen-thousand-member First Baptist Church, Dallas, Texas, and a Fox News contributor. He is also an adjunct professor at Dallas Theological Seminary. He has made more than four thousand guest appearances on various radio and television programs and regularly appears on major mainstream media outlets such as Fox News channel's *Fox and Friends*, *Hannity*, *Lou Dobbs Tonight*, *Varney & Co.*, and *Judge Jeanine*, as well as ABC's *Good Morning America* and HBO's *Real Time with Bill Maher*.

Dr. Jeffress hosts a daily radio program, *Pathway to Victory*, that is heard nationwide on over one thousand stations in major markets such as Dallas-Fort Worth, New York City, Chicago, Los Angeles, Houston, Washington, DC, Philadelphia, San Francisco, Portland, and Seattle. Dr. Jeffress hosts a daily television program, *Pathway to Victory*, that can be seen Monday through Friday on the Trinity Broadcasting Network (TBN) and every Sunday on TBN, Daystar, and The TCT Network. *Pathway to Victory* also airs seven days a week on the Hillsong Channel. His television broadcast reaches 195 countries and is on 11,295 cable and satellite systems throughout the world.

Dr. Jeffress is the author of twenty-seven books, including *Perfect Ending*, *Not All Roads Lead to Heaven*, *A Place Called Heaven*, *Choosing the Extraordinary Life*, *Courageous*, and *Praying for America: 40 Inspiring Stories and Prayers for Our Nation*.

Dr. Jeffress led his congregation in the completion of a $135 million re-creation of its downtown campus. The project is the largest in modern church history and serves as a "spiritual oasis" covering six blocks of downtown Dallas.

Dr. Jeffress graduated with a DMin from Southwestern Baptist Theological Seminary, a ThM from Dallas Theological Seminary, and a BS from Baylor University. In May 2010, he was awarded a Doctor of Divinity degree from Dallas Baptist University. In June 2011, Dr. Jeffress received the Distinguished Alumnus of the Year award from Southwestern Baptist Theological Seminary.

Dr. Jeffress and his wife, Amy, have two daughters and three grandchildren.

A PLACE CALLED
HEAVEN

10 Surprising Truths about
Your Eternal Home

Resources available include...

» The paperback book *A Place Called Heaven* plus "What Seven World Religions Teach about Heaven"—an easy to understand and informative companion brochure

» The complete, unedited series on DVD/CD

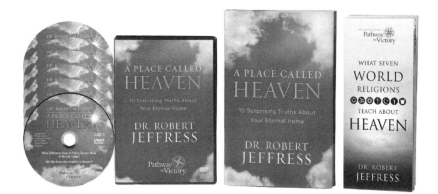

NOT ALL ROADS LEAD TO HEAVEN

Resources available include...

» The paperback book *Not All Roads Lead to Heaven* plus "Christianity, Cults & Religions"—a side-by-side comparison chart of sixteen groups

» The complete, unedited series on DVD/CD

» A comprehensive ten-week Bible study guidebook, complete with answers to study questions and expanded responses to key points

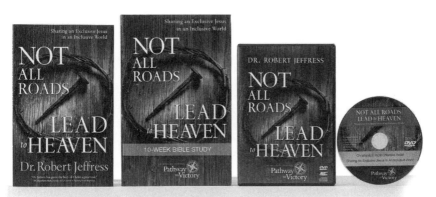

A PLACE CALLED
HEAVEN
FOR KIDS

Colorfully illustrated and using simple concepts and language that children can understand, *A Place Called Heaven for Kids* gives children peace of mind about their lost loved one as well as a comforting, biblical picture of their forever home.

AVAILABLE WHEREVER BOOKS
AND EBOOKS ARE SOLD

Choosing the
Extraordinary
Life

God's Secrets for Success and Significance

Resources available include...

» *Choosing the Extraordinary Life* in hardcover or paperback plus "The Elijah Map"—a companion brochure that shows key events in the life of Elijah.

» The complete, unedited series on DVD/CD

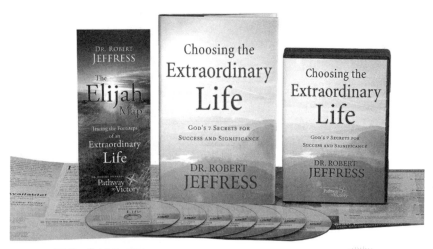